# Voices from Behind the Veil

*Analysis of the Trials, Tribulations, and Triumphs of Middle Class African Americans*

### Michael E. Hodge

University Press of America,® Inc.
Lanham · Boulder · New York · Toronto · Plymouth, UK

Copyright © 2009 by
University Press of America,® Inc.
4501 Forbes Boulevard
Suite 200
Lanham, Maryland 20706
UPA Acquisitions Department (301) 459-3366

Estover Road
Plymouth PL6 7PY
United Kingdom

All rights reserved
Printed in the United States of America
British Library Cataloging in Publication Information Available

Library of Congress Control Number: 2008942466
ISBN-13: 978-0-7618-4525-6 (paperback : alk. paper)
eISBN-13: 978-0-7618-4526-3

∞™ The paper used in this publication meets the minimum
requirements of American National Standard for Information
Sciences—Permanence of Paper for Printed Library Materials,
ANSI Z39.48—1984

*This book is dedicated to my family and especially the memory of my father.*

# TABLE OF CONTENTS

| | |
|---|---|
| Preface | *vii* |
| Chapter 1 Introduction | 1 |
| Chapter 2 Living in America | 11 |
| Chapter 3 American Incorporation | 25 |
| Chapter 4 Marginality in America | 39 |
| Chapter 5 U.S. Cultural Values | 51 |
| Chapter 6 Cultural Opposition | 67 |
| Chapter 7 Conclusion | 79 |
| References | 83 |
| Index | 87 |
| Biography | 89 |

# Preface
## Voices From Beneath The Veil

Mainstream media portrayals would have us see an almost idyllic existence among blacks and whites in the U.S. today. Ostensibly, blacks have overcome the barriers of stereotyping, Jim-Crow, racism and discrimination to mirror their white counterparts. However, every-now-and-again cracks in the bubble show vast discrepancies in the perceived well being between blacks and whites. We see totally different reactions of blacks and whites to the O.J. Simpson verdict--images of the almost celebration of blacks contrasts with the near depression of whites at that "not guilty" verdict. The Washington Post conducted a poll examining the beliefs of white and black males and females about their view of U.S. race relations. Most whites in this survey believe that blacks have equal chances for success; whereas, only 46% of blacks have this same sentiment. These poll results are not surprising and even extend to the science of racial and ethnic relations. I have written this text for a listening and critical audience. That is, readers who are willing to listen to the stories of successful blacks in the society as they negotiate the turbulence of everyday life. And, for those readers who want a careful and critical analysis of these individuals' cases, this book should prove very satisfying. Most of the theories of race relations are not clearly applicable to the African American experience. These approaches tend to assume progressive incorporation into a pre-existing, dominant culture or "mainstream" by a subordinate group.

I focus here on the assimilation process and the marginal personality hypothesis for two reasons. First, these two models work for the majority of White immigrants to the United States. That is, most White immigrants to the United States have come here, faced some discrimination, and been relegated temporarily to marginal, peripheral positions. Eventually, through the ongoing process of "anglicizing" or assimilating to the core American culture, these White ethnics achieved full incorporation. They are on many dimensions indistinguishable from the dominant society members. Secondly, these traditional models form the basis of most analyses of the race relations cycle for American society. They are inherently Eurocentric. They do not consider seriously incorporation of African Americans. They assume no profound and lasting difference in migration's impact and no lasting ideological barriers specific to the experience of African Americans. I argue for a reconstruction of these traditional theories based on the unique experience and history of African Americans.

In order to delineate the dimensions of such a reconstruction of these two existing theories, I rely heavily on the cumulative lived experiences of over 200 African American middle class respondents collected in a national interview. These responses inform a reconstruction of traditional paradigms of Black/White race relations in the U.S. I inject into these theories the experiences of these respondents. Some of the dimensions match the experiences.

Where there are dimensions that do not match, they are rearticulated in light of the experiences of these middle class African Americans.

The experiences of these middle class African American respondents suggest several hypotheses or goals. The experiences used here suggest the need for (1) an Afrocentric perspective of the Black experience; (2) a reconstruction of assimilation and marginality theories to more adequately account for the experiences of African Americans; and (3) a theory of oppositional culture that demonstrates how African Americans are resisting and, indeed are changing, the traditional ways of thinking about Black/White relations.

## *Overview of Chapters*

The introductory chapter provides the rationale for undertaking this work. It lays out the theoretical foundations that form the basis for contemporary race relations. An understanding of these standard canons provides a spring-board for rethinking how such theories are applied to non-white groups within the U.S.

Chapter 2 begins by asking these respondents what it is like to be Black in White America. This chapter is an exploration of the various ways in which African Americans view their life situations given the barriers to full incorporation into the dominant White core culture. This Chapter attempts to identify some of the neo-conservative images of middle class African Americans. The idea that middle-class African Americans do not face racial discrimination is debunked. After these people give voice to their experiences, attention is directed toward the ideological foundations of American core culture.

In Chapter 3 the validity of the ideas of the melting pot ideology, Anglo conformity, and cultural pluralism are explored from the perspective of these middle class African American respondents. The viewpoint expressed by this sample of respondents suggests that none of these assimilation theories is wholly adequate to define the African American situation. These concepts tend to be the main ones articulated in the social science literature. An analysis of the experiences of these interviews suggests a reformulation of the traditional assimilation process that is typically applied to White ethnic groups in America. Injecting the experiences of the African American respondents into these dimensions of the assimilation process produces contradictions to Gordon's analysis. The voices of the respondents in this study will tell their experiences living in American society. The assimilation paradigm is critically challenged by these countervailing data.

Chapter 4 introduces the concept of marginality. I explore the general definition of the marginal personality as explicated by Park and Stonequist (1937). The experiences of the African American respondents are injected into the dimensions of marginality. The voices of these experiences suggest that marginality is something different for African Americans than it is for White ethnics.

Chapter 5 examines the core American values of rationality, strong work ethic, and individualism. How do middle class African Americans view these as values? How are these values modified and used by these respondents? This Chapter forms the foundation of my position that these middle class African Americans are countering the White cultural hegemony that seeks, as these voices attest, to oppress African Americans by suppressing or annihilating their culture.

In chapter 6, I develop the idea of African American cultural opposition. That is, I suggest that African American culture is, in part, oppositional to White cultural hegemony. African American culture offers resistance, both directly and indirectly. Middle class African Americans play a key role in the resistance struggle. Middle class African Americans often find themselves on the front line of the struggle against "the new world order" of modern racism. The duality of being American and African is examined in light of the conflict between cultural hegemony and cultural resistance.

The concluding Chapter summarizes the condition of the African American middle class. Standard assimilation and marginality theories are updated from the perspective of the African American respondents. The oppositional or resistance nature of African American culture that stands in relation to the dominant White American culture is discussed through the components of the Black Power concept (Carmichael and Hamilton, 1966; Hamilton, 1969). The Black Power concept, as explicated by the middle class African American respondents of this study, offers a preliminary Afrocentric reconstruction of African American incorporation.

# Chapter 1
## Introduction

The overall purpose of this book is to offer a reconceptualized Afrocentric perspective to the study of American White/Black race relations. An Afrocentric viewpoint is in order because the most widely used theories of racial and ethnic relations are not directly applicable to the experiences of African Americans. One substantial criticism that can be leveled at traditional race relations theories is that most of these approaches tend to assume that the subordinate group moves toward and inevitably incorporates itself into the pre-existing, dominant culture or "mainstream" society. It is suggested that this ideological perspective forms the foundation of much current neo-conservative rhetoric and policy concerning African Americans. For example, the African American middle class is often heralded by the purveyors of American hegemony as the shining success of the "melting pot" ideal.

I use the term Afrocentric to mean the development of a perspective requiring that African Americans are the central spokespersons for their experiences. The voices of middle class African Americans are heard as they detail and discuss their experiences living in a White dominated American society. There is considerable rhetoric about the success of the African American middle class. The African American middle class is touted as having "made it." In this book, this group of people is given the opportunity to respond from its own particular experiences and vantage points. The popular idea that is held by many White Americans is that middle class African Americans are as well off, or in some cases, better off than their White counterparts. Neo-conservative pedagogues argue support of this notion with data that shows increases in such variables as income and housing desegregation. (Glazer and Moynihan, 1966; Sowell, 1975) Writers such as Steele (1990) use anecdotal personal history and then over generalize to middle class African Americans overall.

This text, in contrast, incorporates in-depth interviews of the lived-experiences of over two-hundred middle class African Americans. They come from a diversity of locales in the United States. These people from many walks of life provide another, not so rosy, reality. The cumulative experiences of living in a White dominated society brings more depth to the all too often shallow and monolithic representation of middle class African Americans. Contrary to the depiction of middle class African Americans by neo-conservative forces, the "experiential" data here indicate that wide gaps remain when analyzing such variables as income, career advancement, neighborhood segregation, and health (Hodge, Dawkins, Key, 2007). The experiences of each individual voice demonstrate that, for each one, racism is a very real part of living in American society today.

## 2  Introduction

I make the argument that traditional approaches for studying race and ethnicity do not adequately or fully account for the African American experience. Thus, by outlining the major assimilation theories, such as the melting pot ideal, Anglo conformity, and cultural pluralism, I show the inappropriateness of applying these models, in their original formulation, to the experiences of middle class African Americans. All of these approaches are models that assume assimilation into the dominant White American core culture. Milton Gordon (1964) outlines this general process. Embedded into Gordon's scheme is the notion that it is proper, expected, and taken for granted that all groups should move and, inevitably, will move into the dominant group. The logical result of this type of worldview creates a standard or a criterion that excludes African Americans from following the assimilation process of most other White ethnic groups.

The White standard follows directly from the notion of Anglo conformity, which has been and continues to be the general model of incorporation and, therefore, success in the United States. This general process is problematic for the African American experience for two reasons. First, the history of African Americans is substantially different from any other immigrant group in this country. Secondly, barriers stemming from this unique history, such as racism and discrimination remain and perpetuate strong opposition to African American inclusion.

Most racial and ethnic relations models posit that incorporation for African Americans has been slow due to structural barriers such as legal segregation. The argument continues, however, that since the demise of these barriers, African Americans are experiencing greater assimilation into the core society. This "progress" is particularly evident among middle class African Americans. Much to the contrary, the cumulative experiences of these middle class African American respondents of this study demonstrate that racist barriers to inclusion remain intact. These barriers require unique responses, at an individual as well as at a cultural level, in order to overcome them.

I focus on Gordon's (1964) outline of the assimilation process and Park's (1937) and Stonequist's (1937) marginal personality hypothesis for two reasons. First, these two models can account for the progression of a majority of the White immigrants in the United States into the core American culture. That is, most White immigrants to the United States have come here and followed the process toward general assimilation. They faced ethnocentrism and varying types and degrees of religious discrimination. They were relegated to marginal, peripheral positions. Eventually, however, through the ongoing process of "anglicizing" or assimilating to the core American culture, these White immigrants were able to achieve nearly complete societal incorporation. They are, for the most part, indistinguishable from the dominant society members. It also seems to me that marginality is the elemental condition for the formation of ethnic enclave minorities and middleman minorities, a factor not discussed in Bonacich's original (1976) analysis.

Secondly, these models form the basis of most analyses of the race relation's cycle of American society. The idea of race relations is complicated by the lack of a clear definition of the term race. O. C. Cox (1948) points out that:

> The term race relations may include all situations of contact between peoples of different races, and for all time. One objection to the use of this term is that there is no universally accepted definition of race (Cox:319).

In order to deal with this dilemma, students of race relations tend to conflate differences in the historical development and presence of racial and ethnic groups. So, immigrant groups are viewed as shedding their cultural heritage and merging indistinguishably into the dominant group in the society. This is the way in which the treatment of race relations between Blacks and Whites has been construed in much of the scientific literature and the popular press, as well. The race relations cycle in America pre-supposes eventual assimilation. Robert Park (1926/1964) wrote that

> The stages of the race relations cycle, contacts, competition, accommodation, and eventual assimilation, is apparently progressive and irreversible. Customs' regulations, immigration restrictions and racial barriers may slacken the tempo of the movement; may perhaps halt it altogether for a time; but cannot change its direction; cannot at any rate reverse it. (Park:150)

These models are inherently Eurocentric. This book considers Eurocentric to mean a worldview that places peoples of mostly northern European ancestry at the center of social analysis. It is where White northern Europeans are used as the standard against which others must measure up. This treatise demonstrates that these Eurocentric models do not adequately account for the general experience of African Americans. Consistently, these theories make the assumption that there is no difference in such processes as migration history, or ideological barriers that is significant from other white ethnic minorities.

However, it cannot be denied that migration patterns directly influence modes of adaptation and assimilation into the core culture. The introduction of African Americans into the core culture is unlike any other group of immigrants. It is the unique experience of African Americans that makes it necessary to refashion these theories. Therefore, I argue for a reconstruction of these theories based on the unique experiences and history of African Americans. The cumulative experiences of these middle class African Americans suggest the reconstruction of assimilation and marginality theories. These experiences articulate an Afrocentric theory for race relations in the United States.

I use a type of extended case methodology to inject the experiences of these respondents into these existing assimilation theories. The extended case method utilizes existing theories that have some explanatory power for the issue under examination. The theories are tested against the data that are the experiences of the respondents. Some of the theoretical dimensions match the experiences; others do not coincide well with the data. The dimensions that do not match are rearticulated in light of the experiences of these middle class African Americans.

The experiences of these middle class African American respondents suggest several hypotheses or goals for the present research. The experiences used here suggest the need for (1) an Afrocentric perspective of the African American experience; (2) a reconstruction of assimilation and marginality theories to more adequately account for the experiences of African Americans; and (3) a theory of oppositional culture that demonstrates how African Americans are resisting and, indeed are changing the traditional ways of thinking about Black/White relations.

Theories of race and ethnicity run the gamut from blending into a melting pot emerging in harmonious homogeneity to celebrating the vast diversity of distinctive cultures to the implicit genocide suggested in some internal colonialism approaches. The problem with most of these concepts is that they do not account very well for the African American experience. Models proffering an internal colonialism framework make some attempt to include them; but these only partially account for the conditions of African Americans in today's society.

## Research Methodology: Indepth Interviews

The study of race relations usually relies upon survey research methodology to define certain trends. The trend data usually provide information about such concerns as the widening income gap between upper class and lower class groupings. The ability to draw on large samples and collect information relatively cheaply using modern telecommunications makes such surveys popular and widely used techniques.

However, the data presented by such methods are surface-level. They do not get to the deeper layers of motivations or concerns of the issue or phenomenon under investigation. There is usually a deeper meaning and motivation to these quick responses. In order to understand these deeper meanings that inform trend data, in-depth, open-ended interviews where the respondent is allowed to freely speak are the most appropriate methodology.

Standard techniques probing middle class African American attitudes of race in the United States would be informative but only at a very surface level for attaining this goal. For example, the major study of African Americans in the last forty years is the National Research Council's (1989) *A Common Destiny*. Most of the data collected for the analysis of *A Common Destiny* was based on survey research data (private and government statistics). Survey research, while offering wide generalizability, loses some of its ability to be able to fully measure the phenomenon in question. Consider the measurement of attitudes. The measurement of attitudes is very complex and as such cannot be accurately assessed simply by using survey techniques. Attitudes that guide behaviors can be understood best by using a qualitative approach. I will briefly outline some of the problems in the utility of data gathered by mass survey techniques. Following this argument I posit that in-depth interviewing of respondents would offer a clearer image of the effects of attitudes on behaviors.

Survey techniques offer very efficient ways of gathering large quantities of data. These data can be gathered across large geographical regions in a cost effective manner by using telephone research organizations, for example. The Census Bureau, of course, uses large mail-outs and a large temporary work force to gather its vital statistics. Mass data collection and survey research definitely have their advantages and are very useful for assessing many relevant issues. However, these various techniques are very broad and become inadequate when applied to more value laden, interpersonal and interactive issues. The method itself commits a type of "attribution error" by over-ascribing causality based on the trend analysis of survey data. The attribution error as described by Kelley (1972) suggests that people will assign more weight to internal characteristics if an outcome is positive. Conversely, people will deny credit if the outcome is negative, and attribute it to external causes. Likewise, mass data collection over-ascribes causality to the probability that a large "random" sample is representative of the general population.

One of the problems is the issue of quantification. Simply, quantification is the assigning of numbers to observations. If appropriately applied, for example, to questions such as asking how many children live in a house, or how many days off from work, quantification increases researchers' agreement on the nature of the observations, increases the amount of information about the observations that can be communicated in a concise way (e.g., census data) and increases the ability to manipulate and summarize observations by making possible the use of powerful tools of mathematics and statistics.

However, to quantify issues of behavioral attribution may be violating the underlying assumptions (such as randomization) of the assignment of numbers. If, for example, I ask people from a random sample to rate on a scale of 1 (disagree strongly) to 5 (agree strongly)—a Likert-type scale—their views on abortion, I discount the attribution processes that went into the development of that rating. In essence, the error that is inherent in the attribution (misattribution) process is compounded by the measurement error of the constraints imposed by the set up of this forced choice questionnaire.

Another issue that creates concerns for survey techniques is the interpretation of the data. The data are numbers that now must be interpreted and extrapolated in order to explain the phenomenon in question. Contemporary social science tackles this task through the use of inferential statistical techniques. Various correlation, trend and regression methods are employed that give some clues to what the numbers are "saying." However, none of these analyses can indicate causality between the variables. Association between the data and the phenomenon is assessed within a certain "probability." Probability analysis, by definition, leaves a certain residual and the validity of the data is determined by the proportional reduction in error (residual) that is accounted for by the data (Agresti and Finlay, 1986). This reduction in error is actually the odds that a researcher will guess, incorrectly, that a theory (or null hypothesis) is correct, that there is no difference between the "actual" population mean and the mean of the sample.

The measurement of attitudes poses additional measurement concerns. First of all, people are reluctant to give information about their true beliefs, especially on sensitive issues with brief questions from a survey researcher. The questions are usually brief, with only a few seconds for understanding and a response. As a rule, survey research allows people to answer without much "soul searching" or thoughtfulness about the question. Answers are often cursory and pallid. In depth interviewing addresses some of the problems associated with survey research.

The chapter in *A Common Destiny* on the racial attitudes of Blacks and Whites relies on survey research data to assess these attitudes. While much valuable information is given, deeper questions of how and why are left unanswered. For example, this chapter concludes with general findings about racial attitudes in America. First, race still matters greatly in the United States. . . second . . . racial attitudes [show] a record of genuine progress. (*A Common Destiny*, 1989:155) It is important to understand why these basic trends occur and how they manifest themselves in the data. A qualitative approach using in depth interviews would allow deeper insight into the actual thinking processes of the respondents. I am not suggesting that survey data is not valuable. On the contrary, I support the use of survey research. However, survey research must be applied appropriately. The survey trend analyses in this chapter of *A Common Destiny* indicate that principles of equality are endorsed less when social contact is close, of long duration, or frequent and when it involves significant numbers of Blacks; Whites are much less prone to endorse policies to implement equal participation of Blacks in society (*A Common Destiny*, 1989:155). In depth interviews would give information on why Whites act in ways discordant with their professed values (the American creed). This more qualitative information would greatly enhance the survey data to provide a more thorough understanding of the attribution of racial attitudes.

## *The Sample: Middle Class African Americans*

The definition of middle class has always been problematic for social analysts. For this study, middle class is defined as those in White-collar jobs including professional, managerial, and high-level technical jobs and those heading up Black-owned businesses (see Landry, 1987). The respondents in this study are teachers, lawyers, doctors, college professors, corporate managers, media broadcasters, business owners, and entrepreneurs, as well as some college students whose parents work in these high prestige type positions.

## *The Extended Case Method*

The problems of survey techniques described above illustrate the importance of qualitative work in the study of race relations. Given this importance, this study incorporated in-depth interviews of middle class African Americans to reconstruct theories of assimilation and marginality. This methodology allows for a deeper level analysis from the particularly unique viewpoint of African Americans about their particularly unique condition in this society. For the present analysis, it is, by definition, an Afrocentric perspective.

One overarching purpose of this study of middle class African Americans is to reformulate existing theories of racial and ethnic relations. The reformulation is intended to be dependent upon the unique life stories of African Americans living, working, and coping in American society. Burawoy (1991) in his publication, *Ethnography Unbound*, makes the argument for what he calls the extended case method. He contrasts this approach with more familiar grounded theory (Glaser and Strauss, 1967) and ethnomethodology approaches. He posits that the extended case method can examine the macro world through the way the latter shapes and in turn is shaped and conditioned by the micro world, the everyday world of face-to-face interaction. (Burawoy, 1991:6)

An interactionist approach tells us that there are reciprocal influences between the individual and the social setting, or between the micro and macro worlds (Fine, 1990). Similarly, the extended case method builds on this very interaction as the nexus between theory development and methodology.

The data, to a large extent, determine what theories to use. Assimilation and marginality theories are central concepts in the study of race and ethnicity. The assimilation process is implicit in the traditional models of inclusion such as melting pot, Anglo conformity, and cultural pluralism. Marginality is posited as a stage through which all immigrants progress toward complete incorporation. The racial, political, and historical experience of African Americans is not treated as "instances of some potential new theory but as counter instances of some old theory. Instead of an exemplar the social situation is viewed as an anomaly." (Burawoy, 1991:9)

## *Theory and Method Interaction*

Let me now briefly describe the anomalies that are exposed by application of the extended case method to the predominant assimilation paradigm in racial and ethnic relations. A further, more in depth assessment will follow in chapter 3. Gordon's (1964) process of assimilation analyzed the movement of immigrant groups into the "mainstream" of American society. He outlines seven sub processes to the general process that leads toward complete assimilation. These processes are cultural assimilation or acculturation, structural assimilation, marital assimilation or amalgamation, identificational assimilation, attitude receptional assimilation, behavior receptional assimilation, and civic assimilation.

Within this framework, Gordon (1964) suggests a paradigm for assimilation in which he analyzes "Negroes", Jews, White, non-Spanish speaking Catholics, and Puerto Ricans. The acculturation of African Americans varies by class. Gordon suggests that the middle class is acculturated because of their more frequent contact with the dominant, White American culture. He also posits that "Negroes" are assimilated at the civic level. African Americans, according to Gordon, have not assimilated on any of the other factors.

Indeed, fi the theory as outlined were demonstrative of middle class African Americans, then the factors on which Gordon (1964) says they are not assimilated would not pose counter instances. But, contrary to Gordon's scheme, the data seem to suggest that there is some degree of incorporation, but only to a point. The conclusions drawn from the logic of acculturation and civic assimilation do not fit the data and partial incorporation seems to be the mode experienced by this sample of African Americans. These data, the cumulative experiences of the respondents, therefore, are anomalies or abnormalities to the theory as explicated. I posit that this partial incorporation produces marginalization as a continual condition of middle class African Americans.

## *Marginality and the Extended Case Method*

Park and Stonequist (1937) make the argument that all immigrants enter a stage of assimilation that is marginal. These immigrants are usually second generation and, in these analysts conceptualization, the immigrants are caught between the cultural values of their native society and the impinging values of the new world society. The ongoing process of assimilation into the dominant core society eventually overtakes this position. Marginality, for White immigrants, has been a temporary condition. However, for middle class African Americans, I argue that their experience of marginality is a permanent condition.

The discrepancies between theory and the reality of experience are seen in nearly every situation with these middle class African Americans. Gordon's (1964) analysis posits cultural and civic assimilation for middle class African Americans. Contrary to this assertion, the evidence presented in this study finds that middle class African Americans have not attained the assimilation stages that Gordon found. For Gordon (1964), acculturation involves taking on the cultural and/or behavioral patterns of the host or dominant society. For example, the adoption of Christianity is seen as proof of acculturation. This book sets as one of its goals the examination of the experiences of these middle class African Americans seeking a clearer definition of this anomaly.

## *Central Concepts: An Afrocentric Reconstruction*

Assimilation is a central concept in the study of race and ethnicity. Theories range from melting pot, to Anglo conformity to cultural pluralism assertions. Each of these concepts implies assimilation into the dominant White American core culture. None of them deals seriously with racial oppression, inequality, or power stratification in U.S. society. Some power conflict perspectives, such as internal colonialism—as put forth by Blauner (1972) in his book *Racial Oppression in America;* offer partial consideration to issues of racial oppression, inequality, and power stratification of African Americans. Blauner argues that the application of traditional assimilation processes to African Americans

> Is based on a number of misconceptions about culture and ethnicity in modern American society. It reflects a restricted usage of the idea of culture and, even more important, a mechanical application of the model of immigrant assimilation to the very different cultural experience of Black people in America. (Blauner, 1972:127)

Part of the problem has to do with the biased nature of the theories themselves. Critically important are the biases of the major theorists. Consider, for example, Gordon's (1964) analysis of the assimilation process. This analysis is probably the most lucid description of the American race relations cycle to date. But, the model is skewed. Gordon's assimilation model is based heavily on the incorporation process of European immigrants into the dominant White American core culture. The model does not consider seriously racism based on skin color, for example, a factor that is unavoidable for African Americans. So, when this model, in its limited form, is applied to African Americans (controlling for class), the results indicate acculturation. That is, middle class African Americans have moved into White neighborhoods, White businesses, White social clubs, and can even make a good-looking run at the presidency of the United States.

A closer examination of this model is needed. It must use the experiences of middle class African Americans is dictated. Theory is best understood through the experiences of those who are living the reality that a given social theory tries to explicate. Gramsci calls these "real" people "organic intellectuals."The organic intellectuals of this study explain their situation as African Americans more clearly and succinctly than any theory to date. The voices of these people define an Afrocentric theory of race relations.

## *An Afrocentric Approach*

Assimilation and marginality are important theories; but they do not go far in assessing the African American experience. The African American experience presents an anomaly for these theories. I set out to reconstruct these theories based on the experiences of the respondents by reference to the wider cultural relations between White Americans and African Americans. However, these data also go beyond Burawoy's methodology in that they suggest an Afrocentric theory of cultural opposition.

The delineation of an Afrocentric theory of opposition, derived from the experiences of middle class African Americans suggests several issues for this research. First, an understanding of the dominant culture is critical. Secondly, African American cultural consciousness is viewed as paramount in maintaining success. This consciousness is demonstrated in the value placed on African retentions (Bastide, 1971; Franklin and Moss, 1989; Herskovits, 1941; Holloway, 1990). And, finally, there is a push for an Afrocentric agenda in areas such as business, education, and in the society at large.

It is important to get an understanding of how middle class African Americans see themselves in American society. I begin with a discussion of how middle class African Americans view themselves in America today. This book is particularly salient given the upcoming presidential election in 2008. As these respondents speak, the reader becomes privy to the often-repressed experiences of covert individual and institutionalized racism. Largely based on a mythological melting pot ideal, and to a lesser degree on the repressed memory of incidents by African American victims, White society has developed insensitivity to the reality of life as African Americans. However, there is an underlying ideological racism that betrays the utopian mindset of White America. This is the dilemma that Gunnar Myrdal (1944) suggested is found between the stated values of the American creed and the instantiation of those values. Racism is forced to be an important part of the everyday reality of African Americans.

# Chapter 2

## Living in America

What is it like to be Black in White America? For many African Americans it is a continuous contradiction. The American ideal of equality and justice for all has proven to be quite elusive for most African Americans. Every move made toward progress by African Americans has been contradicted, in some sense, from fully realizing that progress. It is the fact of this contradiction that is the motivation of this book. Some improvement has been achieved in the 370-plus years of inhabiting the United States; but that progress has not been commensurate with the efforts made.

This Chapter explores the ways in which middle class African Americans view life in the dominant White American society. I begin with a discussion of the image of middle class African Americans. I suggest that this image of success supports the ideology of the great cultural "melting pot." The ideology is one of assimilation or movement into the dominant White American core culture. The "success" of the African American middle class is positive proof of this movement. And, for those who favor American style assimilation, it is evidence that the process works and middle class African Americans have "made it."

After the discussion of the African American middle class image, the voices of the respondents offer insight into the position of African Americans in the dominant society. Experiences of racism and discrimination ranging from housing and employment to restaurants are discussed. The cumulative experiences from the examples demonstrate the racialized nature of American society.

### *African American Middle Class Image*

One ideal image of America is based in the notion of assimilation or incorporation into the melting pot of American culture. The popular idea of the melting pot suggests a blending of cultures that will produce a composite, unique American culture. The general idea of assimilation will be discussed in greater detail in the next Chapter. For the present, it is noteworthy that the "assimilation ideology" sets a standard or goal that all groups must reach in order to be successful in American society. This standard also provides an excuse for the dominant culture. The "mainstream" is divested of responsibility for the condition of the subordinate groups in the society.

For example, the contrasting image of the African American middle and lower classes provides the vehicle for members of the dominant group to argue the merits of the process of assimilation. The pictures of successful African Americans that are generally presented in the media (such as the "Cosby Show" and even the presidential hopeful Barack Obama) and other reports are those of the middle class. The image portrayed is one of parity with Whites. Middle class African Americans have overcome the stagnation of low income and the cycle of poverty and as such are more respected by Whites and they are accepted into the same arenas as their White counterparts. Some conservative writers, some of which are Black (Steele, 1990; Sowell, 1987) have suggested that this trend indicates that racism has been buried and that the society is color blind in its relations to African Americans. The general understanding, then, is that middle class African Americans have integrated and they have been assimilated.

This notion of a colorblind society was strongly bolstered with the Supreme Court's conservative renderings on race conscious programs. These rulings are basically counterproductive in our racially and ethnically diverse society. Other scholarly work has argued in the framework of assimilation. Glazer and Moynihan (1963), for example, make a strong push for "Negro assimilation." They write that:

> All the work of incorporating Negroes, as a group and as individuals, into a common society--economically, culturally, socially, politically--must be pushed as hard as possible (pg. xxiv).

There is a cadre of co-opted African American neoconservative scholars who to write about a type of "enemy-memory" of racial oppression. They argue that the communal memories of slavery and segregation are turned into enhanced myths and conspiracies of an overly powerful racism than actually exists today. These types of proclamations are indicative of the current trend of neoconservative thinking that has shaped racial and ethnic relations nearly a half-century in this country. However, the perceptions of middle class African Americans, as they live in the dominant White American society, construct a different reality.

Each incident of racial discrimination is interconnected with each incident in the life history of the respondent as well as to the larger community of African Americans experiencing similar conditions. Each incident should be viewed as a snapshot of a long and continuing record of assaults against individual African Americans and the larger community. These snapshots illustrate, contrary to the prevailing neoconservative rhetoric that these middle class African Americans continue to face discrimination based on race. The following sections will demonstrate, through the recollections of these respondents, what it is like in contemporary American society. The perspective of these middle class African Americans will indicate the continuing significance of race in their lives.

## *Living Black in America*

What is it like being a middle class African American in the United States today? From the worldview of African Americans, the reality is bitter sweet.

The bitter reality is that African Americans perceive their continued exclusion from access to equal opportunity as racially motivated (Feagin, 1991). For example, a railroad company employee acknowledges that limitations are set upon her and her family based solely on race.

> For me and my family I would have to say that it's maybe two different viewpoints. For me I find it frustrating. I find it very frustrating to be a Black in America today because I am aware of the challenges, I am aware of how far I've come, but I am also aware that it's a long way to go. And it's not a matter of, it's due to things that I can't control, i.e, my color. It's not a matter of me being a nicer person, or a more aggressive person, or more assertive person, or doing the right things. I think the biggest barrier is my color.

A state legislative aide points out the idea that African Americans have learned how to suffer. He views the terrain of Black and White racial relations as virtually unchanged from the era of legal segregation.

> I don't think it's very different than it ever has been, it's just living hell. I think, who was it that said, to be Black in America is to be in a constant state of rage. I think that's pretty accurate. It's kind of like we've learned, we haven't learned how to stop suffering, but we've learned how to suffer peacefully.

The sweet reward is found in the progress that has been made by some African Americans since the 1960s Civil Rights movement. An academic advisor in a large state university system acknowledges the progress made by African Americans in business, politics, and education. She believes that:

> To be Black in America is not necessarily a negative thing, as Blacks have developed in many ways, in many significant ways professionally, politically, and academically. And therefore, even though we have quite a few more strides to make, considering the strides that we HAVE made, I find that being Black in America is not a bad experience, and it is, to the contrary, a very positive thing.

A student who works part time as a hospital technician feels that being Black in America is good. However, even this optimistic assessment is tempered by a sense of racial discrimination. This respondent relies on a strong idea of African American heritage to fortify him against self-doubt and a negative self-image.

> Well, for me personally, I think it's good. Because throughout my life, since I had the ability to perceive reality as it is, I've always been taught good values in life, to respect myself, to respect others. I was exposed to the history of my people at a very early age, and that gave me a lot of self pride, and gave me the mental strength to battle the negative forces that I would say have been executed against me because of my race. And as a result of that, I've been strong enough to counteract that and not to break down or have some type of

negative image of myself, a self hate of myself, because I've always been knowledgeable of myself and my people, where I come from and what I want to do in life. That alone has been the driving force to keep me going and struggling against a quote, unquote, racist society.

## *Listen to Voices Yet Unheard*

There is a feeble stability in the position of middle class African Americans, a safe call is somewhere around 22 percent of African Americans occupy a loosely defined position of middle class. The respondents in this study meet the income levels for middle class. However, income levels alone are not always the best measure of middle class status. In addition, the prestige of people's occupations enhances their status as middle class. This study considers middle class as White-collar jobs including professional, managerial, and high-level technical positions (see Landry, 1987).

The excerpts already exposed and those in the sections that will follow are from teachers, dentists, physicians, college professors, corporation managers, ministers, media personnel, and students whose parents occupy these high prestige and income positions. The important point here is that these people spend great amounts of time interacting with Whites who also occupy these types of positions. Therefore, the experiences reported by the respondents are not encounters with extreme racists such as the Ku Klux Klan or skinheads, for example. Many of the reported encounters are with highly educated, well paid Whites that these African Americans have to deal with almost daily. In order to answer what it is like to be Black in White America today, the voices of those who live that reality are heard. W. E. B. Du Bois (1903) wrote that African Americans are

> Different from the others; or like, mayhap, in heart and life and longing, but shut out from their world by a vast veil . . . The Negro is a sort of seventh son, born with a veil, and gifted with second sight in this American world, --a world which yields him no true self consciousness, but only lets him see himself through the revelation of the other world.

The veil is very thick and the voices of the masses are rarely heard. The following interviews offer a forum for those voices that need to be heard. The voices of these middle class African Americans are heard from beneath the veil.

As previously mentioned, neoconservative proponents have asserted that racism has been over-run by class issues as the major concern of the exclusion of African Americans. The rhetoric of these neoconservatives suggests that proof of the death of racism is seen through the incorporation of Blacks into some of the institutions in the society and the subsequent growth of the African American middle class. However, from the recollection of their own incidents living in White dominated America, this sample of African Americans presents a different analysis.

To begin, consider the following respondent. Countering co-opted spokespersons, a veteran schoolteacher responds simply to assertions of a weaker, more diluted racism. Her experience is beyond the popular rhetoric of African American incorporation and ideals of having "made it."She knows the continuing struggle to obtain the guaranteed rights (privileges) of citizenship in this country.

> To be Black in White America these days is very much like it was in those days. There are some privileges going to us that we have long fought for that are long overdue that we now enjoy because of our efforts, not because of anyone else other than Black Americans. We are now enjoying some of the privileges that we earned long ago because we were part of the history making of America.

She uses the economic condition of her family to indicate the hard battle to maintain middle class status. Her husband and she both work; but her son also contributes to the income to maintain their standard of living. This is the condition for most African Americans. Their standard of living is very tedious and unstable.

> For my family and for me, economic conditions are somewhat better because of a united effort. As for Black Americans, we are still depressed economically, we are still depressed culturally, and we are still deprived culturally. Some things have been achieved, but we have a long way to go. We have made a lot of progress, but we both work. We have one son, he works, to achieve what we have, which is really an average living condition. It's a united struggle for all of us.

A program consultant for a large aerospace company describes her situation of being Black in a predominantly White environment as "a constant challenge, day to day, in keeping your mind focused on being competitive, keeping your spirits high in order to maintain a positive outlook, when you know situations, in many cases, are stacked against you…"This respondent views her assessment of life in America as a challenge to face the odds that are weighed against African American success. Another respondent who is a counseling psychologist at a major university stresses the point that Black life in White America is a struggle against feelings of loneliness and isolation. These feelings are part of the struggle to exist.

> Well, some days it's a really day to day struggle to exist. Some days, it's lonely being Black in America. Lonely being Black where I work, on campus. And there seem to be fewer days when it feels really ok. It still feels very much like a struggle to show evidence that I'm, that we're worthy in this society. It's still a struggle.

The belief held by many Whites that middle class African Americans have fully assimilated into the mainstream has resulted in the policy direction of the last decade. Historians Franklin and Moss (1989) point out in their chapter on "New Forms of Activism" that long standing, precedent setting anti-discrimination legislation has been seriously curtailed and in some instances reversed. These respondents are very much aware of these trends.

For instance, a minister who has risen in the ranks of the Methodist Episcopal Church sighs his assessment of the trend of the Reagan and Bush administrations. The neoconservative wave has actually pushed the civil rights progress of African Americans backwards. It is a direct result of the deep-rooted belief in the assimilation process working successfully for middle class African Americans.

> I don't see them getting any better. Now, I don't mean to be pessimistic, but with the Reagan/Bush Court and the latest three or four decisions that they have reinterpreted, we have gone backwards. And I don't see Mr. Bush having the backbone to really do anything about it with the executive office.

Some of the more blatant consequences can be seen in the resurgence of anti-Black hate groups and crimes. During the 1980s there was an upswing in the visibility of the Ku Klux Klan and other White supremacy groups such as "skin heads" and neo-Nazis. Also, lawsuits were filed and won by Whites alleging reverse discrimination. Courts have tended to side with anti-affirmative action proponents in viewing reparation or indemnification programs such as set asides, goals and quotas as unconstitutional. These facts contradict the seemingly near utopian depiction of the situation for middle class African Americans.

Neo-conservative rhetoric about the insignificance of race has been the ideological foundation for much of the expressed attitudes of Whites towards African Americans for the last decade and continues to be a major driving force in the 21st century. Holding fast to a belief in the American ideal of assimilation, the causes of inequality are refocused onto the disadvantaged group.

The myth is not the Black paranoia intoned in the idea of an "enemy-memory." This type of discourse constructs a mythical relationship that is not supportive of, in Berger's and Luckmann's (1977) terms, the "objectivated reality" of the society. For instance, neo-conservative discourse argues that many Whites face discrimination because of affirmative action in college admissions. That is, there is an instance of what has been called reverse discrimination. On an individual basis, a few Whites may be able to point to instances where they may have been slighted. However, if a more global approach is taken we can see that the greatest proportion of institutional funds go to White students. Data show that while 64% of White students receive aid only 42% of Black students receive the same type of aid. The objectivated reality negates the predominate myths about affirmative action and reverse discrimination.

The discourse between so-called liberal and conservative perspectives of the urban underclass can be distilled to an emphasis on the level of analysis. Liberals have the tendency to focus on how the problems of disadvantaged groups are related to the conditions of the broader society. The variable of interest, then, is the rates observed in these social dislocations, such as rate of crime, and rate of illegitimacy. Conservatives tend to emphasize the importance of group values and competitive resources, such as underdeveloped work ethic, preference for illicit activities to work, and preference for welfare. Liberals are more apt to analyze the problems of the urban underclass in structural societal terms; whereas, conservatives are more apt to examine them in more individualistic motivational terms.

Within the framework of conservative discourse, language such as pathology, antisocial behaviors, and maladaptive behaviors, are used to suggest that the basic reasons for the plight of the urban underclass rests solely with the inability of the "subculture" to assimilate into the mainstream society. This perspective implies that the poorest people (and African Americans, in particular) are in their peculiar predicament because they are engaging in behaviors that are not acceptable to the mainstream society, and these behaviors are directly and vicariously taught to the children and "passed down". Hence, the culture and cycle of poverty are perpetuated. Even the use of the word "underclass" has come to mean that the "analyses tend to blame the victims by focusing on the subculture and attitudes of the Black poor and excoriate liberal government programs for creating ghetto dwellers without a work ethic" (Feagin and Feagin, 1990:122). This philosophy, by default or by design, sanctions and legitimizes the laissez-faire actions of the government and private sectors alike. However, if these perspectives are viewed from an Afrocentric perspective, the differences merge. An Afrocentric perspective indicates that both views assume eventual incorporation into the dominant White American core culture. And, hence, both arguments are moot because of barriers to assimilation that are faced by African Americans, no matter what their class status.

## A Racialized Environment

The racial attitudes of most Whites, being the dominant social group, make it difficult to obtain racial parity for subdominant groups in the society. *A Common Destiny* (1989), in the chapter "Racial Attitudes and Behaviors", stresses the disequilibrium that is established between the values White Americans profess to hold in high regard and their behaviors under conditions where those values are tested. More than fifty years ago, Gunnar Myrdal asserted the same basic premise of discordant values and behaviors. Myrdal's epic study, *An American Dilemma*, suggested that the behaviors of the American people were incongruent with the stated ideals of the nation; i.e., the American Creed. The American creed is based on the notion that "all men are created equal and are endowed with certain inalienable rights."As Myrdal concluded in 1944, and it is still true today, there are discrepancies in the stated policy of the United States and its actions.

Living in an environment that is racialized has definite and deleterious effects on African Americans at all status levels. The data from the Black middle class respondents in the present study indicate clearly that they are not exempt from the ravages of a racialized society. Consider the following excerpt that intensely identifies the status of African Americans in a racialized society. This respondent is a highly educated and well-paid entrepreneur. By all outward signs, she has "made it." She makes a shocking statement that captures the severity of the oppression experienced by a lot of middle class African Americans. She replied that it's "like one step from suicide." This self employed business consultant goes on to say that living in a racist society "has created a mental health problem. It's a wonder we haven't all gone out and killed somebody or killed ourselves."

There is no where a more vividly tragic representation of the ravages of living in a racialized environment than the idea of giving up the struggle, not just the racial struggle, but the struggle of just living. Kevin Early (1992) argues for the buffering effect of the African American church and African Americans strong belief in the immorality of suicide. However, when the conditions become so unbearable, when the images of that support appear like the "enemy," even the strongest may break.

Contemporary American racism is more complex and covert than that of the recent past. Yet, evidence of racist attitudes and actions can be found in nearly every corner of American society. Middle class African Americans view the existence of racism and race discrimination as an ever-present reality. At the least, they have to prepare to deal with it on a daily basis--at work, at school, walking down a street, in restaurants and in service stations (Benjamin, 1991; Essed, 1990, 1991; Feagin, 1991). For example, the following respondent relates the experiences she had while looking for a house to rent:

> But I think one incident that made an impression on me was a woman answered the door when I came to look at a house. This was to rent. And she just laughed, just started laughing when she saw my Black face, and closed the door in my face, and didn't even respond. Yes, she was the owner of the house.

Not only did this respondent receive this blatant discriminatory treatment from an individual homeowner, but also she received similar treatment from a realtor who did not know she is Black:

> And I had a woman tell me on the phone that I would like the neighborhood because there were no Blacks in it, and I said, "Well, my dear, you're in for a big surprise, because if I buy it, there will be a Black there then, because I am now. I am a Black."And she gasped, you know, and just hung the phone up.

While these types of blatant exclusionary tactics of the recent past may have subsided, we see that these types of incidents remain all too common. The racism exhibited was not intended to be blatant. It just happened that the White realtor could not determine this woman's "Black" voice.

James Scott (1990) discusses the "use-value" of hegemonic discourse. In this case, the power of racism is circulated "backstage" in its rawest form; whereas, public discourse is more "politically correct." Yet, the public display is only the surface of much invidious hegemonic or dominant power relationships. Whites assume the more powerful position and develop an ideology to support the established standard against any and all incursions. Baker (1992) refers to this relationship as maintaining the homogeneity of the state line against heterogeneic eruptions of that status quo.

Similarly, in the first incident, the landlord simply refused to have anything to do with this Black person. Momentary heterogeneity on the part of the dominant party, in this case, rudely laughing and slamming the door as if to say, "I can't believe you had the nerve to come to this White neighborhood--surely you know better" is necessary to maintain social distance and the connection of the superiority/inferiority relationship. The incident with the realtor underscores the pervasive belief among many White business people that African Americans somehow degrade things with which they have any contact. The realtor, believing that the person on the phone was White felt no hesitation in saying that the neighborhood is nice because it has no African Americans living there. Out of all the positive attributes that could sell a house, this fact was primary. Again, establishing the power and dominance of White racism among those of "kindred hearts" in its private rawness perpetuates the dominant group's ideological stance. On a more basic level, it is important to notice here that there is no indication that the landlord or the realtor had any concern about the respondent's ability to pay or to meet any other qualifications. Racial category and the associated racist ideology were sufficient to exclude this respondent from even the opportunity to compete for these houses. Race is the master status.

Middle class African Americans also perceive certain limitations to success because of race. A young Methodist minister points out that the system is set up to perpetuate discrimination. It is designed to maintain the homogeneity of the status quo. He contends that no matter what "At this stage of the system, at this point I'm not going to become bishop." The reality that is perceived by this respondent is one of limited upward mobility. It is not just for him but for his wife as well. He gives an example of an African American minister that ran for bishop of the area for the United Methodist Church. Note the attitudes that seemingly direct the behaviors of Whites toward the possibility of having an African American in this highly prestigious and authoritative position. The impression is that it is alright for Blacks to have the "opportunity" to be included, but that opportunity cannot be turned into reality.

> The United Methodist Church has the best promising career of any Black in [this city], in terms of the United Methodist Church. He ran for bishop last year and withdrew his name in the first or second round, because Whites just won't be supportive. There's a whole area of the conference that said, "We don't want this man, because we don't feel like a Black man can handle our conference, so he can run for bishop here, but we don't want him here." And we still live in a system that gives lip service to equality and fairness and justice, but the bottom line is that White people have never consciously and intentionally looked beyond our skin color to see what we have to offer, whatever we're doing. It has to be an intentional thing. They don't see you or me, and say this is a talented human being and I want that. No, they say "he's Black, but" or "she's Black, but." There's an exception. So to be Black and be successful contributor is to be an exception to what White folks see in other Black folks.

Contrary to the rhetoric of neoconservative commentators, the experiences of these respondents point to the fact that the significance of race has not declined. Race does matter.

## Challenging Everyday Racism

What does it mean to be Black in a White dominated society? This was the first question posed the respondents in our sample. Racism and discrimination are part of the experiences of most responses to this question. Ostensibly, these middle class African Americans have "made it." They have somehow slipped the surly bonds of poverty. At the same time, there is an image that this release from poverty has transformed these people. Middle class African Americans, supposedly, are accepted as equal in White America. Middle class African Americans, particularly, have moved from their marginalized position. They have been assimilated and are doing well economically and socially.

However, the vast majority of these middle class respondents relate experiences of racism and discrimination that they face all too often. These middle class African Americans speak and inform an Afrocentric theory through their experiences of the reality of what it is like for them "living in America."

These middle class and upper middle class African Americans indicate that racism and discrimination interdependently affect their daily lives. The cumulative experiences betray ideas suggesting that African Americans are overly sensitive or paranoid. For these people, neo-conservative thinkers are miserably out of synchrony with their proclamation that anti-Black racism is not as strong today as it was in the past. An experienced teacher summarizes the definitive response to these cohorts when she states that: "[America is] still as racist as it ever was, but we're just a step closer to doing something about it."

A private practice attorney assesses his experience. For him, the situation for African Americans is the same as before civil rights legislation. He states that it is

Probably no different than it was fifty years ago. Essentially, racism is a problem in our society, and Blacks have been the victims of racism and racial oppression. The form of our oppression, the form of racism has changed over the years, but the existence of it cannot be denied, and it exists today. So I guess, succinctly put, I feel like a victim of some of the American institutions.

The responses from most of the respondents, like the attorney above, indicate that they continue to face discrimination, but in a more covert and sophisticated form. Middle class African Americans perceive racism and discrimination as very much alive and operational in American society; but in its more sophisticated manifestations new strategies are necessary for dealing with it. A respondent indicates the covert sophistication of contemporary racism when applying for a job:

Certain cues such as attitudes exhibited by the White employees that indicate that the incident was most likely race based... but you just never know. But I just never knew. You know, I found out some of my other friends who got hired who's stuff wasn't as strong as mine, and judging by the reaction that I would get when I would walk into an interview, you know, the whole floor would seem to just stop, to see this Black man in a tie walking in with a portfolio as if he actually wants to do something besides being a janitor. It makes you think maybe the color of my skin is a *big* factor in me getting or not getting this job.

The complexity of the social setting tends to obscure the underlying motivations for certain behaviors. As this respondent points out it is difficult to know—is it truly a lack of satisfactory credentials; or, is it skin color, like this respondent's gut reaction tells him?

This type of attitude leads to a number of misperceptions concerning the effects of anti-discrimination programs and the ineffectiveness of government programs. A student at a private college describes the covert nature of racist attitudes that Whites exhibit in their comments and queries:

My major concern is just the institutionalized racism; the racism that's not so visible. The racism that's just that gnawing, smoldering type of racism that happens that makes people say, "Why do we need an    Office of Minority Affairs? Why do you *need* Black professors?"That type of racism that springs from ignorance and racism just springs from habit. Everyone knows not to call Black folks "niggers" anymore. Everyone knows that, but everyone doesn't see the importance of Black professors, Black people in places of power. It'd be a whole different college if everybody who served the food here at this university was White, and everybody who taught the classes was Black. Then I think a lot of White people would see—but that's never gonna happen, so.

The complexity of contemporary racism also obscures the reality of the gap in racial equality. The Black middle class has made considerable economic gains since the civil rights era. However, a closer investigation points out the widening gap between the African American middle class and the White middle class. These data offer conflicting information to the dominant idea proffered by the mass media and some social science reports that hard work is all that is needed to succeed in America today. The value of hard work is part of the cultural foundation of the American ideal. The image is that African Americans and Whites live harmoniously together in equality--as long as African Americans work hard. Hard work may be an understatement of the effort that must go into maintaining middle class status as an African American.

McAdoo (1981) points out that many Black middle class husbands often maintain their level not only by using a second working person in the family but a second job as well, generally on a part time basis. Our sample of middle class respondents expresses this necessity in their own situations. For instance, a university administrator from a large northeastern city describes what her family had to do to be able to afford the mortgage after experiencing difficulty (some of it racial discrimination) in renting a house: "Then I decided that I was going to buy a house, so I worked two jobs so that I'd be able to buy a house, and saved the money from the second job to be able to buy the house with, because it took all the money from the first job just to live."

Another respondent indicates how both husband and wife must work and sometimes take on additional work just to maintain the fragile barrier between middle class and working poor African Americans. This respondent sees the real possibility of losing a job to racism. So, African Americans must work hard to maintain a modest standard of living.

> The White boy will take your job just as quick as you can blink your eye, and all of that [material possessions and status symbols] means nothing. If anything you're so out there in hock, that you will shortly be back where your momma and daddy came from, if not sooner. I think so many people are struggling just to survive, because they do have that standard of living, because they do want a nice place to live and that costs money, they do want nice groceries, they do want nice clothes. Not really anything extra, but just to keep that standard of living means working two jobs in some cases, wife and husband working.

An administrator for a public school district captures the essence of trying to maintain middle class status in an environment that denies access to equal opportunity. In spite of the fact that they are highly educated and exhibit all the prerequisite credentials, African Americans are not able to attain equity with their White counterparts. Even for middle class African Americans, acculturation does not fit the experiences of these respondents.

> Well, it's hard for us to maintain the standard of living that we would like to maintain, or reach the standard of living that most White people have because we're not afforded the opportunities to be employed in certain job positions that would afford us a higher grade of living. And I'm not just speaking about my husband and myself, I'm speaking of my family at large. Even though they

might have skills that they've been trained for, they all have college degrees, it's just impossible for them to be employed in certain positions that would afford them the high standard of living that we all would like to have. But White people in the same category that we're in don't face that problem.

Consistent with the earlier respondent's experience of the united struggle to maintain, these middle class Black Americans have a clear sense of the fragile nature of their status. This fragility is not just within one family, but it is experienced throughout many families and even the African American community.

African Americans experience the advantage going to Whites in low employment and tough economic times. They understand that educational attainment is no guarantee of commensurate reward, as it usually is with Whites. So, hard work to the extreme is the norm for many middle class African American families--just to maintain a modest standard of living. Racism and discrimination exist and even those middle class Black Americans who work hard find that their status is tedious at best.

The state legislative aide that was heard earlier, very aptly describes the condition of contemporary life for African Americans. He describes working in the legislature and the thoughts of the policy makers that affect African Americans.

> What is it like to be Black in America today? It is a living hell, working in this environment, in a political environment, in a policymaking environment; you get to see the raw nuts and bolts of how this country really works. You see that all the lofty rhetoric about freedom, justice and equality and democracy is all a joke, the whole process from beginning to end. The whole process from beginning to end is controlled by, of and for a certain sector of American society, the corporate moneyed sector, and they don't make any bones about it down here. There are no illusions about it, that's just the way it is.
>
> I've looked at this society for a long time from a lot of different viewpoints, and I've studied and I've read and I've tried to understand, and I think I do understand to a certain extent, so I don't expect anymore. I think the frustration comes in, and I do get frustrated sometimes, but I think for most African Americans, those who are so-called middle class especially, I think the frustration comes in when, ... We see it every single day in the corporate sector, in the political sector, economic sectors like, ... we fight like hell to learn the rules of the game, we fight like hell to make the team, we finally make the team, then we fight like hell to get in the starting line up, then we fight like hell to get our turn up at bat, and then finally when it's our turn at bat, then boom, they change the rules. And that goes on every, single day. This is just a racist country, pure and simple.

## Summary

Middle class African Americans have not escaped the sting of racism and discrimination. Racism and discrimination are experienced in housing, education, restaurants, and in employment. The cumulative nature of these experiences and their occurrence across cases supports their validity. All of these experiences are barriers to incorporation into the mainstream. I will now turn attention to the process of assimilation that forms the standard for success in American society. The route to assimilation creates its own paradox vis-à-vis African Americans.

# Chapter 3
## American Incorporation

The "ideal of America" is its own paradox. The paradox is found in the idea of inclusion and acceptance while the very process excludes certain groups within this nation. The notion of the colorblind society that is current in race relations discourse is similar to "melting pot" ideas about America's ethnic immigrants. The rhetoric of a colorblind society implies that structural functionalist conceptualizations of the assimilation process have been successful.

Du Bois (1903) pointed out that the problem of the 20th century is the problem of the color line. Assimilation for African Americans has not been the same as it has been for other groups of Americans. It is important to understand the differences as well as the similarities of African and White Americans in the process of incorporation.

This Chapter begins with a description of the major race and ethnic models. These models, melting pot, Anglo conformity and cultural pluralism are examined in light of data provided from the experiences of middle class respondents. These models, for the most part, envision a one-way movement into the mainstream or dominate White American culture. The data from this study suggest that these assimilationist theories lack explanatory power when applied to African Americans. The foundation is prepared for an Afrocentric reconstruction of these models.

After this introduction to the major assimilation models, assimilation as a process is defined. Then Gordon's (1964) assimilation paradigm is generally examined and then applied to the experiences of the middle class African American sample of this study.

### *Models of Assimilation*

Assimilation in American society is a perplexing and complicated issue that is beyond the simple coming together of different ethnic groups. The issues effect the everyday relations of differing groups of people. Noblesse notions of freedom, justice, equality, and the land of opportunity bring the mix of peoples in the United States together. Intrinsic to these ideals are the American cultural values of individualism, work ethic, and rationality. These ideals are represented in the words of poet Emma Lazarus emblazoned upon the pedestal of the Statue of Liberty:

> Give me your tired, your poor,
> Your huddled masses, yearning to breathe free,
> The wretched refuse of your teeming shore,
> Send these, the homeless, tempest-tost to me:
> I lift my lamp beside the golden door.

These different peoples bring with them heavy cultural baggage from the "old world". What happens when all these different peoples interact? How do they reconcile potentially conflicting worldviews? Social scientists have tried to study these issues and offer some understanding to the developing patterns. In the following pages I offer a brief description of the major assimilation models that are used to explain the intermixing of different peoples within the United States.

## Assimilation defined

Assimilation can be generally defined as a process or act of making an object similar or adapting an object to another. More socially definitive and useful for the present purposes, Robert Park and E.W. Burgess (1921) defined assimilation as the "process of interpenetration and fusion in which persons and groups acquire the memories, sentiments, and attitudes of other persons or groups, and by sharing their experience and history, are incorporated with them in a common cultural life."

This definition underscores several important factors. First, assimilation is a process. As a process, people move through stages or phases toward what Park and Burgess (1921) call "its final perfect product"—assimilation. Secondly, assimilation involves deep level intermixing and combining. This suggests ethnic and racial intermixing such as intermarriage and multiracial and multiethnic offspring. And finally, these first two stages will lead to a perfectly homogeneous society where racial and ethnic differences are blended away.

This definition has been very influential in guiding the thinking of American sociology. Many writers on these issues tend to follow this general tradition. They posit, generally, a one way blending of newcomers into the already existent, White-Anglo-Saxon-Protestant host society. Park and Burgess state that through the process of assimilation newcomers "are incorporated with them (i.e., Whites and Protestants) in a common cultural life." The basic models of assimilation allow for none or insignificant reciprocal contributions to the host core society. None of the models of the assimilation process adequately address the case of African Americans in this society.

## Melting Pot

The United States has been popularly praised as a sort of melting pot of the world's cultural diversity. Irving Zangwill wrote a play based on his conception of immigrating to the U.S. He writes that:

> America is God's Crucible, the great Melting-Pot where all races of Europe are melting and reforming! Here you stand, good folks, think I, when I see them at Ellis Island, here you stand in your fifty groups, with your fifty languages and histories, and your fifty blood hatreds and rivalries. But you won't be long like

that, brothers, for these are the fires of God. . . . A fig for your feuds and vendettas! Germans and Frenchmen, Irishmen and Englishmen, Jews and Russians-- into the Crucible with you all! God is making the American.

The melting pot theory of assimilation posits that immigrant groups entering the United States will eventually "melt" into the brewing stew of all other groups thereby forming a new breed called "the American." There would be a disappearance of distinctive minority groups as well as the host society into an all new "fused" society and culture. In other words, the core of the host culture would be substantially changed along with the immigrant group.

Clearly, Park and Burgess (1921) had this type of notion in mind with their definition of assimilation as "a process of interpenetration and fusion."Further, one of the most persuasive arguments offered for the notion of America as a melting pot was by historian Frederick Jackson Turner. He explains that the dominant influence in American institutions was not the nation's European heritage alone, but the experiences of the Western frontier of the United States. McLemore (1991) explains Turner's viewpoint that:

> The western American frontier functioned as a great leveler of persons and a blender of cultures. . . . The new American culture that arose on the frontier contained significant contributions from the various cultures but was distinctly different from any of them"(pp. 60-61).

A closer reading of the excerpt from Zangwill's play reveals the exclusion of immigrants of color. He speaks specifically about Europeans ("where all the races of Europe are melting and reforming!"). Clearly, African Americans were not even considered in his assessment. Furthermore, the events described are toward the White, northern European American image. America as God's crucible could only make something in the image of God-- that is, of White northern European stock.

The idea of the American melting pot supports the ideal of America as being the land of opportunity, freedom, and justice. However, just like the ideals out of which this model is derived, actual experience falls far short of the goal. For example, an examination of the western frontier shows that truly there are certain unique features that can be attributed to a "blending of cultures" on the westward trek. However, the majority of the underlying motif is, nevertheless, European. The direction of the blending is toward the White American standard with heavy influence on northern European traditions.

## *American Ideal: African American Reality*

The model of the United States as a type of melting pot does not fit the reality of the general American experience. I am not arguing that this inadequacy of the process is a condition found solely among African Americans. The process is not adequate for most other immigrants as well. Other immigrant groups like the southern Italians and European Jews have faced barriers to incorporation. What I do argue, however, is that the experience of African Americans in relation to the pressure toward assimilation is wholly unique. Forced immigration and enslavement and the development of an ideological racism to support and rationalize this system of exclusion (Cox, 1946), creates an experience that is qualitatively different from other immigrants to the United States. Schermerhorn (1970) pointed out in his typology of coerced migration that slave transfers are the most coercive type of migration. And, further, Kitano states that:

> Among all of our racial minorities, Afro-Americans (or Blacks, or Americans of African ancestry) have suffered the longest and the most. They have been and continue to be the principal victims of racism: the primary objects of prejudice, discrimination and segregation. (Kitano, 1991:97)

Formidable barriers are in place against African Americans for the type of incorporation that other "White" immigrants possess. African Americans are prevented from melting into the general stewing pot. While the nation touts its lofty ideal of equality of opportunity, many African Americans are barred from full societal inclusion. The voices of those impacted must be heard. So, hear middle class African American "organic intellectuals" as they formulate their Afrocentric theory of experience in American society.

The legislative aide, encountered in the previous chapter, is worth hearing again. The ideals that are held up as America do not come to African Americans with the same meaning. "All the lofty rhetoric about freedom, justice and equality and democracy is all a joke, the whole process from beginning to end."

It is important to understand, and I drive the point, that these are the actual lived experiences of these people. This legislative aid is not speaking about something he heard second or third hand. He is relating information that he has seen and heard from his close, day-to-day contact with Whites who are in powerful decision making positions.

Another respondent, a television broadcaster speaks succinctly to the hypocrisy of American ideals.

> This country is such a hypocrite when it comes to talking about the melting pot. What melting pot? What melting pot? If you're White you're over here, if you're Black you're over here. There's no melting pot, there is no melting pot in this country.

Historical experience that has become part of the "stream of consciousness" of African Americans and the everyday experiences of living in White America have conditioned their responses. The ideals of rightness, justice, and equality are strongly supported values of African Americans. Exclusion from basic opportunity structures in the face of these ideals necessarily structures the worldviews of African Americans. A student at a major university lays bare the sham of integration into the dominant White American society.

> And speaking socially, you have to always be cognizant of the fact that the bulk of White America will never accept you totally, basically because this nation is so race conscious, Black Americans are always fighting a battle with racism. I mean, it is everywhere; it is ingrained in our system. It's ingrained in the system that's supposed to be so beneficial for us, integration. I mean, integration's supposed to be, at least I thought it was supposed to be a system where we would learn from their culture, they would learn from our culture, we would intertwine the two cultures and become one.

This astute respondent makes clear that the melting pot notion is not applicable to African Americans. She is aware that deeply ingrained institutional racism is the cause of exclusion of middle class African Americans from the opportunity structures available to their White counterparts. Her experience and those of the other respondents in this study (and countless others) form their reality that is drastically different from the popular notions espoused by the "American Creed."

A self-employed petroleum industry consultant views the condition of African Americans to White Americans as a power relationship. The hopefulness that Whites will willingly relinquish some of this power is cynically punctuated by laughter. She does not see Whites relinquishing their power hold. She does see the necessity of African Americans taking more control.

> I guess, (laughs) I guess, I'd like to see us become a part of that society, and so therefore, if you start out with one hundred percent, they now have eighty, they can get sixty if we can have forty! (laughs) I don't put the total blame on them. See, power is funny. They are in the positions to make power decisions, and they're not going to make a whole lot of power decisions that will diffuse their power. They don't want to give up power that they still have some control over. We have to recognize that the Supreme Court has one Black, and when he dies, lord knows when we'll get another one.

African Americans must assume responsibility for leading the charge to gain inclusion into the society.

> I just don't think we're doing enough. There are so many things that we have to assume responsibility for, and to sit and say, the White race ought to change or they ought to do that, they're not going to do a thing until we make them do it. It may have to go beyond turning the other cheek, and being passive, I would hope not, but for us to get equality, in the truest sense, we're going to have to take some drastic measures. And I don't see us doing that, and I don't see the White race letting us in. So, I don't see the White race doing anything, I see the Black race assuming more responsibility to catch up, economically, academically, politically.

The above respondent states it well when she says that the White race will not let African Americans into the mainstream.

An operations manager for a large data services corporation sees the melting pot ideology as presenting a false sense of accomplishments. He feels that eating in restaurants and other civil rights accomplishments have tended to lull people into a mythological world of equality.

> I think we've taken some gains, which we've tended to take for granted at this point. We feel like because we can now go in and sit down in a restaurant next to a White and eat a meal and we don't have to go upstairs in a movie theater anymore and we don't have to go to the back of the bus to ride the bus that we've reached a level of equality. We live in neighborhoods now that we used to not be able to live in, so we feel like that we've arrived. So in that sense, we're living under a false sense of accomplishments, and I think that there's a lot of work to be done with regards to skills, salary equity, career growth and development. In other words, we're still being blocked out of the main thrust of society, and we've got to continue to expect more than what we're being allowed to have.

This respondent captures the sentiment of many African Americans who feel they are blocked from the main thrust of society. They do not melt into the American crucible. The reality for African Americans is not an intertwining of cultures, but an expectation and a thrust toward conformity--Anglo conformity.

## *Anglo Conformity*

The basic tenet of an Anglo conformity model of assimilation is that peoples coming to the United States are encouraged and expected to shed their old world ways and adopt the White Anglo-American value-belief and behavior systems. The more fully immigrants are able to take on the ways of Anglo-American culture, the more accepted and eventually successful they become in the society. In essence, this type of assimilation is seen as a process in which the immigrant eventually replaces the old world culture with the new Anglo-American pattern of life and standards of behavior.

Contrary to the melting pot idea, Anglo conformity does not suggest that the host society is changed in any way. It is the core Anglo, White American culture that immigrant groups are expected to adopt and embrace as their own. The experience of immigrants to the United States indicates that an Anglo conformity model fits more closely with the actual experience of the peoples of America.

This "standard of behavior" is an important concept that will be dealt with in greater detail later. However, for the present purposes, it should be understood that it is generally impossible to reach the standards totally. Hence, Anglo conformity, and indeed, all forms of assimilation, is a matter of degrees. The greater one's ability to shed distinctive language forms, religious practices, and behavior patterns the more readily incorporation into the mainstream, dominant society is achieved.

It is these very standards that shape the present status of White/Black relations in the United States. For example, while it can be shown that the African American middle class has attained a modicum of success vis-à-vis a type of assimilation total acceptance into mainstream White society is yet to occur. The following respondent, a student at a major university, demonstrates the pressures to conform to the dominant, White society. She stresses that inclusion simply means to be White. And, unlike the "melting pot" ideal of Zangwill, the Afrocentric perspective deriving from a unique historical experience does not offer the same analysis.

> Black Americans are always the ones that are expected to adopt the White culture. . . . That's not really what I consider integration. . . . To integrate means simply to be White. It doesn't mean fuse the two cultures, it simply means to be White, that's all. . . you're just constantly forced to take on the culture of White America.

The director of a school library system summarizes the plight of African Americans in face of pressures to conform and their continuing exclusion.

> We're all supposed to be equal, have equal opportunities in all phases of life, even though it's not true. . . all things are NOT equal, even though we say that they are. Blacks are still in a subordinate kind of position because it doesn't matter what position you're in, it's not a position of power. You're still in a subordinate position just by virtue of being Black.

The Afrocentric viewpoint of these respondents suggests that there is great pressure to adopt White cultural values and behavior patterns in order to be accepted. This Afrocentric perspective, contrary to Park and Burgess (1921), does not suggest that there is any "process of interpenetration and fusion . . . or a common cultural life." The problem with the assimilation process is that there are barriers that have been erected to prevent African American inclusion. These barriers remain institutionalized and formidable. One of the barriers is the inability of African Americans to shed their skin color. They cannot become "invisible" within the social milieu, even if desired.

## Cultural Pluralism

The basic premise of this approach to assimilation argues that each ethnic group has the freedom to choose the degree of assimilation. They would be allowed to retain as much or as little of the "old world" culture as desired. McLemore (1991) points out that "in short, the pluralist minority wishes to be equal to the majority in all matters affecting citizens but nonetheless to maintain its separate culture and social life"(pg. 63).

Cultural pluralism as a concept is of relatively recent vintage. However, pluralist minorities always have been a part of the American experience.

The notion is somewhat confused by competing positions of its proponents. McLemore (1991) offers an attempt at clarification. He divides cultural pluralism into assimilation by substitution and assimilation by addition. Substitution refers to pluralist minorities accepting the Anglo culture as the standard to emulate. For instance, a minority group will become bilingual. They will function in the majority of their daily existence as fully assimilated and their native language becomes secondary. In other words, they have substituted Anglo culture for a great portion of their distinctive cultural expression—language.

Assimilation by addition, on the other hand, refers to pluralist minorities exerting and expressing their native cultures in their everyday lives. Not only would some minorities become bilingual, but majority members would become bilingual. In other words, American English would not be the only national language--in fact, there would be no national language. Any assimilation toward an Anglo culture would be by taking on or adding to the basic foundation of their old world culture.

Greeley (1974) has offered another variant of the cultural pluralism model. He has coined the term ethnogenesis. Ethnogenesis refers to the process whereby people from the same nationality or religious orientation form a new religioethnic group within a different society. This model suggests that there are major native retentions that play critical roles in the daily lives of the new group. In essence, there is a creation of a new ethnicity that is dependent upon the conditions in the host society.

These distinctions still leave some concern about the true differences between cultural pluralism, melting pot and Anglo conformity perspectives. The issue simplifies to the fact that the predominate system within American society is White, Anglo-Saxon and Protestant. All of these models run into similar problems. The experience of the United States indicates that there continues to be a power differential with Whites controlling the majority of the resources of that power. And, further, "it has generally been the lot of groups with less power to adapt to changing realities" (Kitano, 1991:25).

In a summation, it is important to note that the models of assimilation just outlined imply, generally, a one way process. That is, an eventual movement into the so-called mainstream society. This movement entails, by definition, a "giving up" of most of the previous values, practices and traditions of the native culture and replacing them with the new ways of the host society. Gordon (1964) writes that: "The price of such assimilation, however, is the disappearance of the ethnic group as a separate entity and the evaporation of its distinctive values" (pg. 81).

None of the models deals adequately with the situation of African Americans. For most "voluntary" immigrant groups, the process has not been wrought with the deep rooted barriers to incorporation based on ideological racism. Ethnic, cultural, and religious differences are often eclipsed by "Whiteness" as a common denominator (see Gleason, 1980). Gordon (1964) points out that for the White immigrants the acculturation process was only delayed by such things as ethnocentrism and religious conflicts. But its ultimate victory was inevitable.

For African Americans the process is much more difficult. Racism and discrimination figure prominently into the process of African American incorporation into American life. Gordon (1964) tries to come to terms with this failing in his approach by suggesting that the problem of African American acculturation since the end of de jure segregation is largely a class problem. He believes that the African American middle class is the same as all other immigrant groups--they just have some catching up to do; but, they are basically indistinguishable in behavior patterns from middle class Whites. Citing religion, he concludes that since the overwhelming majority of African Americans are Protestant and some are Catholic, there are no significant differences between African American and White American worshippers. He goes on to state that "the Negro is developing a middle class indistinguishable in basic behavior patterns from middle class Whites. . . ."(pg. 108) In a footnote, Gordon makes the argument that the middle class is distinguished from the lower African American classes because of the latter's isolation from middle class White Americans. However, he states, "middle and upper class Negroes . . . are acculturated to American core culture"(pg. 76).

The conceptualization of assimilation in the United States can be seen as a type of metamorphosis. Just as a caterpillar eventually evolves into a butterfly, so too are newcomers to evolve into "Americans."Biologists speak of the phenotype and genotype of a species. Phenotype mainly refers to outward appearance. Genotype refers to specific gene characteristics that are considered unchangeable, except through evolutionary mutations. Species are most reliably identified by their genotype. For example, genotypically, the butterfly is still a caterpillar. But, phenotypically, it looks and acts much differently than it did in its former state.

Assimilation into American society implies a change in the actions, speech, behavior, customs and even appearance of the newcomer. Immigrants must mimic the mainstream standard as closely as possible. White immigrants can phenotypically alter themselves, even though they retain the basic genotype. African Americans cannot alter all of their phenotype markers from the genotype basis.

## *The Anglo American Standard*

Milton Gordon (1964) provides one of the most lucid depictions of American style assimilation. He offers an analysis of the assimilation process as consisting of seven variables with two variant goal-systems (pp. 69-75). He spends considerable time discussing the reciprocal influence of immigrant culture upon the White, Anglo-Saxon and mostly protestant core culture. However, he eventually concludes that: "It is quite likely that Anglo conformity in its more moderate forms has been the most prevalent ideology of assimilation in America throughout the nation's history"(Gordon, 1964:75)

The previous discussion concludes that Anglo conformity is the general mode of assimilation. It is also the standard toward which others must strive and the standard by which others are evaluated. More than this, Anglo conformity carries with it a notion of Anglo (White) superiority.

White northern Europeans came to the "new world" of the Americas in search of new economic opportunities. Throughout the centuries, these Europeans managed to secure domination numerically and politically. From the inception of the Republic, laws were written to secure the rights of landowners. The original constitution provided protection to the landowners giving them the exclusive right to vote. Later, laws were passed limiting the number of immigrants into the country. These acts, and others like them, helped to solidify the power hold of the White Anglo-Saxon Protestant (WASP) group within this new society.

O.C. Cox (1948) noted that the rise of the Anglo-Saxons to their position of power could be traced to capitalistic exploits of the Europeans. With religious fervor and economic greed, Anglo-Saxons began to travel the world in search of riches. Eventually, these exploits came to the "Americas". The new lands were colonized and the indigenous peoples expelled, enslaved or destroyed. Cox shows how capitalist interests developed the ideology of racial antagonism and the subjugation of people of color. He remarks that

> The exploitation of the colored workers... consigns them to employment and treatment that is humanly degrading. In order to justify this treatment the exploiters must argue that the workers are innately degraded and degenerate, consequently they naturally merit their condition. (Cox, 1948:334)

Anglo American dominance became established as early as the 1690s in the American colonies (McLemore, 1991). The standards by which all others coming to America would be compared were established in the image of the dominant White Anglo-Saxon, Protestant group. The extent to which someone was to be considered American or not American was based on a comparison to this dominant group. This "attitude" on the part of Whites naturally supported their beliefs in their inherent superiority over African Americans. It provided the economic satisfaction and the moral justification to continue a system of oppression and denigration.

## *Gordon's Assimilation Process*

Assimilation is a process toward full inclusion and participation in the society. It was discussed earlier that conceptualizations of this process take several forms. The forms include popular ideas of a melting pot society, conformity to dominant, White existing standards, and various pluralistic approaches. Gordon

(1964) offered a detailed analysis of the general process of assimilation. In this classic treatise, he theorized seven stages in the process toward what Park and Burgess (1921) call "that perfect condition"—assimilation.

Gordon sets up a hypothetical situation of two groups of people, the Mundovians and the Sylvanians who have to interact with each other at some level. The Mundovians immigrated to Sylvania and are in the process of assimilating into the host (Sylvanian) way of living. These variables are not necessarily time ordered in that they do not necessarily occur in the sequence in which they appear in this hypothetical case. In this hypothetical case, the Mundovians move toward that perfect condition of the Sylvanians by first acculturating. Acculturation involves changing cultural patterns such as religious beliefs and practices and speech patterns and dialects in order to match the dominant host society as closely as possible.

The next stage is generally structural assimilation. This stage involves the inclusion of the new group in many of the dominant group institutions. Yetman (1985) refers to this stage as secondary structural assimilation, noting that it is limited to impersonal types of interaction such as schools, businesses, social clubs, and the like. A deeper interaction is amalgamation or what Yetman (1985) calls primary structural assimilation. For Gordon, this is marital assimilation which is characterized by large scale intermarriage. The logical conclusion to this type of assimilation is the production of multiracial and multiethnic offspring which would eventually result in no racial differences.

Prolonged contact with the dominant host society encourages identificational assimilation. This stage is characterized by the development of one's sense of people hood based on the dominant society. In other words, the immigrant begins to more closely identify with the host society than with the "home" or "old-world" culture. Attitude receptional assimilation refers to the absence of prejudice toward the newcomer. And, behavior receptional assimilation refers to the absence of discrimination toward the newcomer. It seems to me that both of these stages are actually extensions of the earlier stages of assimilation. There may not be an actual absence of prejudice and discrimination. The newcomers may be so identified, now, with the host society that they are insensitive to the more subtle and covert actions toward them. Finally, there is civic assimilation. It is the absence of value and power conflict.

## *African American Assimilation Process*

Gordon provides a paradigm of the assimilation process for various racial, ethnic, and religious groups in the United States. Assuming the goal of adaptation to the core, dominant Anglo society and culture, none of the groups listed has completely assimilated (Gordon, 1964:76). He analyzes the African American (Negro) position in the model. He suggests that African Americans have reached civic assimilation. They have also attained acculturation depending on their class level. Middle class African Americans are more acculturated than lower class African Americans because of the differences in frequency of contact with White society. In all other stages of assimilation, African Americans have not adapted. There are several problems with the explication of Gordon's model when it is applied to African Americans.

How do African Americans view their position in the United States? Do middle class African Americans view themselves as acculturated as suggested by Gordon? Do they believe that there is not any conflict of values between African American culture and White American culture? The data herein contradict most of the assertions implied by Gordon's model and they suggest a different interrelationship between African and White Americans.

For instance, most of the middle class respondents do not view themselves as fully integrated into the American society. A graduate student explains that: "You can never fully integrate into a society that is unwilling to appreciate or respect who you are and what you stand for." Another respondent echoes the same experience with the assimilation process. She says that "speaking socially, you have to always be cognizant of the fact that the bulk of White America will never accept you totally. . ."

The African American middle class, in particular, faces a constant clash of values. This conflict becomes the focus of the marginal status of the African American middle class. A respondent views it as a struggle to gain second or third class status in America. The ideas of a melting pot do not stand the test of the experience lived by African Americans. And, conforming to the White standards does not provide the promised rewards for African Americans. The promise of freedom, justice, and democracy eludes the experience of African Americans.

> Racism is still alive and really well, and there's just a struggle to perpetuate second and third class citizens instead of trying to really put forth the effort to make all these people here first class citizens. We seem here to be much more concerned with making other countries of the world democracies than we are making our own country a democracy. So I don't know whether we are going to get back on the track and move more toward being a real democracy or whether we're going to keep on being hypocrites and try to talk about making the world a democracy, while at the same time we make a joke of democracy in our own country.

These respondents indicate their frustration at having to be acceptable to Whites in order to be successful, and, at the same time, trying to service the African American community. It is like an analogy given by a respondent on the differences perceived by being associated with one group or another. She says that even when

> you look at something as simple as just a group of people talking, Black people are given a much higher regard if they are seen in an all White group than if they were to be seen in an all Black group. If you're seen in an all White group laughing and talking, you're seen as a respectable, and probably

taking care of something important, you're not wasting time, you're alright. But if you're in an all Black group, regardless if they can even hear your conversation or whatever, White people think you're trying to, you're congregated to take over the world. It's just that basic, even an association, you're just punished for expressing your Black culture, be it just being with other Black people, you're just constantly forced to take on the culture of White America.

A principal for an urban school district relates the process of assimilation into White American culture as frustrating.

There seems to be so many "tests" that must be passed on a daily basis. Meritorious effort does not carry over from event to event simply because of stereotypes held by Whites about the competence of African Americans. I'll have to say as James Baldwin once said, "To be Black in America is to live in a constant state of frustration."And you have to always prove yourself. And no matter how competently you perform today, tomorrow you start off with a clean slate, because you're Black. To prove again the next day that you are competent. As if the White man is saying, "Yes, you did well today, but that was by pure accident. I want to see how you're going to do tomorrow."And it's a constant process of proving your competency. They will not accept Black competence nor Black authority or leadership.

The popular commentary is that middle class African Americans have fully incorporated into the mainstream society. However, as this vice president of student services for a major university system points out, the cost is much greater for African Americans than it is for their White counterparts. He knows that to maintain that middle class status, African Americans must

often times forth a greater effort to succeed than your White counterpoints. This is something I've dealt with for years, ever since I've become a professional, and I guess I've even dealt with it before that time, in attending public schools and competing in high schools or activities. It's always been like that. I see that as sort of a given.

It will be seen that African Americans are offering an alternative to being "forced to take on the culture of White America."Through cultural opposition, African Americans are providing a challenge to the status quo hegemony of White America.

## Summary

In this Chapter, I have attempted to demonstrate that an understanding of American style assimilation is an important starting point for understanding Black and White race relations. The general tendency has been to view the assimilation process for African Americans as either one of no difference; or, at most temporarily slowed by structural barriers such as dejure segregation of the recent past. However, the voices that have been heard thus far indicate that this process is more than postponed. The assimilation process, in its original form, does not apply to the condition of African Americans. The data from these respondents indicate that African Americans still face barriers that place them in perpetual marginal status to the dominant White culture.

In the next section, I detail Stonequist's (1937) marginality conceptualization. I make the argument that because of continuing racism and discrimination marginality is a permanent condition for African Americans and not a stage on the way toward societal incorporation.

# Chapter 4
## Marginality In America

### *The Marginal Group*

Marginality is an old concept that was coined by Everett Stonequist in the late 1930s. However, the idea probably has its germination in the works of W.E.B. Du Bois around the turn of the century. Marginality as a concept in the social science literature has typically been applied to immigrant groups that attempt to assimilate or "melt" into the mainstream or dominant culture.

This usage was the contribution of Robert Park and Everett Stonequist (1937) and describes the conflict experienced when role expectations of the dominant host culture or "new world" contradict past roles and behaviors of the immigrant newcomer. The greater the extent to which the new world roles are incorporated into the personality of the newcomer, the greater will be the acceptance of the newcomer by the dominant host culture. A person or group is said to be marginal or on the outside of accepted norms if the newcomer is not able to incorporate the new roles. By definition, then, the marginal person or group is deviant. Park asserts that membership in incompatible social groups leads to a "deviance-prone" condition known as marginality.

Immigrant groups have suffered from this type of categorization at least since the 1890s in this country. For example, most of the Italian immigrants came to the U.S. hoping to make fortunes and return to Italy. Therefore, many of them held tightly to their traditions and customs. When this return did not happen many were not able to fully assimilate into the Anglo American culture (McLemore, 1991). Consequently, they were in contrast to the dominant cultural system.

The inability to totally adopt the Anglo-American standard will result in a group that is considered deviant or outside the norms of society results from. In the United States, the foundation of that standard involves the reification of the American cultural values of individualism, work ethic, and rationality. If a group has disproportionately high unemployment rates for example, then the group is seen as having a poor work ethic. This condition, which is probably the result of a number of structural factors, including racism and discrimination, is generalized to the entire group. They are stereotyped as lazy, shiftless, and, of course, criminal.

### *Stereotyping and Marginality*

The connection between stereotyping and marginality has not been directly studied. Ziller, (1954) suggests on the psychological manifestations of the marginal personality that the root cause may be social and not psychodynamic.

Thus, some of the available social psychological literature suggests that there is a relationship between marginality and stereotyping. This relationship is instructive for the present analysis. It adds clarity to the position that the dominant core culture uses stereotypes to place and keep a group in a marginal position. Stonequist (1937) and Park (1937) did not anticipate this relationship in their analyses. Walter Lippmann (1922) was the first to observe that stereotypes are provided by the particular culture. The dominant culture will issue positive stereotypes about itself and negative stereotypes about subordinate groups in and out of the society. The relationship to marginality and assimilation is clear. The more assimilated a group is to the dominant culture, the less negative the stereotypes, and the less assimilated a group is to the dominant culture, the more negative are the stereotypes. These negative stereotypes serve to assert the authority of the dominant group. Negative stereotypes are generally degrading, if not downright dehumanizing. Negative racial stereotypes of subordinate groups are one means of asserting the authority of the dominant group. Hence, the non-assimilation of this group of immigrants fostered the development of widespread stereotypes and prejudices.

Italians were called such derogatory names as "wops," "dagos," and "guineas." The slums in which they were forced to remain were seen as veritable dens of crime and delinquency, with much attention given to the so-called "Mafia" or "Cosa Nostra." Even today the "mafia" and other crime syndicates are generally stereotyped as Italian or "Sicilian" based. Despite these stereotypes Italian Americans developed an emergent ethnicity (McLemore, 1991:94-95) that has been quite successful within the United States. Other ethnic minorities (mostly European) similarly have been able to form a distinct ethnic identity that is viable within the dominant Anglo American society.

This process of assimilation is consistent with Gordon's (1964) typology. By the second or third generation, the continuing process of assimilation has eclipsed marginal status for White immigrant groups across all the variables. Movement toward the dominant American core culture reduces the negative stereotyping. Old world customs and values have been replaced and identificational assimilation is deeply ingrained and solidified.

Many immigrant groups have an impact on the core culture as well. A pluralistic model that suggests a more equity based exchange or interaction between cultures has been posited by Greeley (1974). He refers to this process as ethnogenesis. In the case of Italian Americans, the co-exchange involves both a movement toward the American core culture while at the same time, some Italian customs are picked up and expressed by the core society. An example might be the strong influence of certain Italian culinary patterns that is found expressed in some of the cuisine of the core American society.

## Slavery and Marginalization

African Americans present a unique situation. Unlike the Italians, or most other European groups, Africans did not freely immigrate to the United States. They were brought to this country against their wills for the sole purpose of being labor for wealthy landowners. Cox (1948) points out that Africans were brought here as slaves for cheap labor. Color had nothing to do with the original use of Africans as slaves. Race as some type of abstract, natural, immemorial feeling of mutual anti-pathy between groups began solely as a justification for the cruel and inhumane treatment inflicted upon the slaves. Thus, a rationalization for the contrasting positions of Anglo Christian ethics and plantation slavery had to be developed. I note that the "American dilemma" (Myrdal, 1946) is as old as America—slaves just were not in a position to make anything of the inconsistencies.

There were many slave rebellions and uprisings. Herbert Aptheker (1943) reports over 250 slave uprisings and conspiracies within the continental United States. One the most dangerous jobs was to be an overseer, for there was a great probability of being killed in the fields by slaves. Also, plantation owners had a legitimate fear that their property would be destroyed if they left it for any length of time. Lerone Bennett challenges the "persistent myth of the docile slave."Slaves were not the happy-go-lucky, docile creatures oftentimes portrayed in American history. On the contrary, there were repeated insurrections and there is solid evidence that the South lived in constant fear of the "docile" slaves. (Bennett, 1961:91)

A core tenet for Christians is to love everyone and others as one would want to be treated--"Love thy neighbor as thyself"(the Ten Commandments). Since this was not occurring, the White, Christian slave holders had to develop some rationalization or justification for their behaviors. These behaviors are out of synch with their Christian faith and ideology. The solution to the quandary was that slaves were to be considered savages and subhuman and "innately degraded and degenerate, consequently they naturally merit their condition" (Cox, 1948:334). It was also the duty of a good Christian to "Christianize" the world and save the savages from their hell-bound ways. Thus, the bringing of the Africans to America as slaves was in line with saving them from sure eternal destruction. This part of the ideology eventually caused problems when Christian abolitionists used it against the slave owners.

However, once the original rationalizations were solidified, the pattern developed into an ideological driving force based on the belief in the innate inferiority of Africans because of their "savage" nature and dark skin and the innate superiorities of Whites. This ideological stance developed and was perpetuated for centuries and indeed is embedded into the very fabric of this society. Beginning as capitalistic exploitation for a cheap labor supply linked to a moral justification for continuing cruel and inhumane treatment, ideological racism became one of the cornerstones of the culture of the dominant American society. (Wallerstein, 1989)

## The Marginalization of African Americans

White Europeans, and some other immigrant groups, if they so chose, were able to "lose" themselves through some type of ethnogenesis (Greeley, 1974) where these people are able to form a hybrid culture of remnants of the "old world" with "new world" values and practices. For some, it was as simple a matter as changing or "Anglicizing" names; for others it was a more difficult task of shedding distinctive cultural accents and dialects. African Americans, however, have always stood out by virtue of physical characteristics. Names or dialects do not matter, skin color is all that is necessary to distinguish and set apart Black people from the mainstream society. Du Bois (1903) states it succinctly: "the problem of the twentieth century is the problem of the color line."

In terms of marginality, then, African Americans are placed and kept on the outskirts of society. And, African Americans, more than any other immigrant group in America, remain peripheral to the mainstream, central society. Lurie (1982) states: "Immigrant communities were usually not communities when they came; their ethnic identities were, to a surprising extent, constructed in America." The key is that the ethnic identity construction is allowed of these groups. Schermerhorn (1970) points out that slavery, as a type of migration, was the most coercive and destructive type. The forced immigration of Africans to America was followed by direct and vicious attempts to destroy their cultural and ethnic identity because of ideological racism and the belief that somehow these people were less than human.

African Americans are caught in the middle of the conflict of the ideals and the reality of White Americans. White Americans defend their ideals and belief in the American creed by alleging that African Americans do not want to become an integral part of the society. Yet, many refuse to acknowledge and change existing structural barriers that would grant more African Americans access. This long-standing ideological racism was clearly demonstrated in the 1899 ruling in the *Cumming* case rendered by the U.S. Supreme Court. The unanimous opinion, delivered by Justice John M. Harlan, set the stage for outrageous discrimination against African Americans in education. The Court's earlier ruling in the *Dred Scot* case adds further credence to the culpability of the deeply ingrained ideological racism. It was not until 1954 that this dejure segregation was outlawed.

However, the foundations of the deeply rooted ideology of racial oppression remain even today. Black Americans have struggled for centuries to be recognized and accepted in the mainstream of American society. The ideology of racial oppression and discrimination has thwarted many of the efforts of the

Black masses toward these ends. Truly, the continuing problem of the twenty first century is the problem of the color line.

Gunnar Myrdal wrote in the 1940s that the dilemma of American society must be viewed as not acting in the interest of the stated ideals of American democracy. That is, America symbolizes the ultimate of democratic values; but it is hard pressed to enact measures to ensure these basic rights for all of its citizens. White Americans today appear to be less prejudiced and espouse lofty democratic ideals of equality and egalitarianism. At the same time, they oppose policies that would put these ideals into practice and actually ensure these values for all American citizens.

For example, the majority of White Americans state that they would have no problem living in a neighborhood that has a Black resident. But, when asked how likely they would be to live next door to a Black family, the majority report little likelihood that they would do so. Most Whites say that African Americans should not be discriminated against in the work place but they are against affirmative action policies. This juxtaposition of stated values and action on the part of White Americans goes above and beyond the notion of some type of idealistic dilemma in democratic philosophy.

## *Privilege and Marginality*

The examination of marginality indicates that along with the use of stereotypes to assert dominant White hegemony, a hierarchy of privilege is established as well. Marginal groups are not privileged in the dominant society. Whites in America have lived with advantage and privilege for so long that it has become something that is taken for granted. Most White people in America do not know that their actions may be racist and discriminatory. Most White Americans operate at a sort of half-conscious or subconscious level of racism (Aleinikoff, 1990). When the respondents of this study mention instances of contested discrimination, they report that most of the Whites are taken aback, taken off-guard and did not even think their actions were offensive. Racism is so embedded and so conventional for many Whites in this society. It is rarely challenged so many Whites may never think of their actions as racist.

Living a privileged status has made most White Americans insensitive to the condition of other subordinate groups in the society. African Americans have been relegated to subordinate social status in this society. Racism and discrimination have systematically excluded them from the mainstream of American opportunity structures. When African American middle class respondents are asked what they would most like to see changed in American society, a great many responses are in reference to the insensitivity of Whites. For example, a psychologist sees some of the things White people do as just simply

> Down and out insensitive. Some of the things that my colleagues do that are insensitive. One colleague—I refused to work with him because he was very patronizing. I just said, I won't work with you under these conditions, and I backed out of the project. I had to preserve my own integrity. He was an elitist. And he had a hierarchy in his mind of where people belonged... I was at the bottom of that hierarchy, not having talents and skills, and he having all of the wisdom, and wanting to impart that to me in a kind of one directional way. Failing to think that I might have something to offer him.

This African American's exemplary experience points out the power position that members of the dominant cultural group assume because of their privileged vantage point. The ideological racism supported by negative stereotypes and the imposition of dominant cultural values is parts of the insensitivity of advantage and privilege. This privilege is not isolated to obscure or remote individual actions. It is pervasive and is manifested in the oppression experienced in the everyday lives of African Americans. A veteran business executive explains the problems he faces with the privilege established through continued marginalization of African Americans.

> So, in other words, in spite of the fact that you've been able to, happened to mainstream institutions and acquire mainstream American knowledge by way of some of the in ways in which most Americans, or at least most White Americans, make use of mainstream institutions and values, even though you acquired this knowledge and then did service to your country and got college and graduate degree level work, you still weren't treated the same as others? And in addition to that, it goes even beyond that. Once you point out the treatment that you're receiving and you use the established procedures to have it rectified, it results in further adverse treatment. The assumption is that my detractors, the White males that I was dealing with, it's an implicit assumption on their part that they have the right to do what they were doing and that I have no right to complain. And should I complain, rather than listen and deal with it in a positive way that will get past the problems, the intent is to go into a very elaborate defensive position, and in so doing will actually prolong the problems.

African American marginality does not form a "middleman minority" culture. Middleman minorities develop from being able and being allowed to satisfy certain economic needs of the society. Bonacich (1973) used the term "sojourning" because these immigrant groups did not have the intention of staying in the United States. They were here to amass as much capital as possible and return with it to their homelands.

African Americans are not sojourners. Some have been able to claim their niche and make returns to the community. John Sibley Butler (1992) has labeled such entrepreneurs the truncated middle class. Most African Americans, however, have not been able to own their own businesses. Marginality for African Americans is not a sojourn. Marginality is an imposed condition where, until relatively recently (the past 25 years), African Americans were excluded from all but the most menial of jobs. With the advent of Civil Rights legislation, some progress has been made.

One of the most visible indicators of this progress is the development of a significant Black middle class. Some of these African Americans pursued careers in government positions and a few managed to land some corporate middle management level positions. Access to higher educational opportunities also added to the pool of candidates for a developing African American middle class. While much of this change was occurring, African Americans were still alienated from the mainstream.

Middle class African Americans remain a marginalized group. They are tangentially recognized but not granted full access or participation. Commensurate with economic and other opportunities African Americans began to obtain college degrees in greater numbers. They began to get degrees in areas that were historically reserved for White males. However, civil rights gains provided some inroads. Houston Baker (1991) points out that the barrier is breached and the flood is inevitable.

## Marginality and Racial Solidarity

The analysis of marginality by Park and Stonequist (1937) indicates that the marginal personality develops a type of self-hatred. Identificational assimilation (Gordon, 1964) can be seen not only as taking on the cultural values of the dominant culture, but also as a rejection of the native culture. The self-hatred induced by marginal status is manifested in the denial of the native culture.

These theories are inconsistent when this analysis is applied to middle class African Americans. Black Consciousness is on the rise, not in decline, among African Americans. It will be shown in a later section that the respondents in this study place great importance on the development and expression of both the African and American components of their heritage. Briefly, the sample of middle class African Americans understand their duality as a result of being marginalized. Park and Stonequist (1937) indicate that the marginal personality is that with a more "rational" worldview. The rationality of middle class African Americans is created from the reality of having to understand White culture and use it to make some headway in this society. But, marginality also requires African Americans to entrench themselves in the African part of their culture. Du Bois (1903) captures the very essence of this solidarity of consciousness:

> It changed the child of Emancipation to the youth with dawning self consciousness, self realization, self respect. In those somber forests of his striving his own soul rose before him, and he saw himself, darkly as through a veil; and yet he saw himself as some faint revelation of his power, of his mission... the spiritual striving of the freedmen's sons is the travail of souls whose burden is almost beyond the measure of their strength, but who bear it in the

name of an historic race, in the name of this the land of their father's fathers, and in the name of human opportunity. (Souls of Black Folk: 12-14)

## *A View From the Inside*

Marginality for African Americans is a permanent status that is characterized by exclusion, insensitivity, invisibility, and negative stereotypes. It is, as one respondent stated, "a struggle to survive." The struggle is to resist cultural (and physical) annihilation. Does the African American middle class see itself as marginalized, or on the outskirts or periphery of full participation in American society? The following excerpts indicate the way this sample of middle class African Americans views its relationship to mainstream American society. The struggle is using marginality and the co-existent biculturality as an offense and a defense against White cultural hegemony.

A student living in a large southwestern metropolitan area interprets her feeling of isolation, the feeling of being there but not really allowed to participate fully (tokenism):

> A lot of things come to mind, I think about isolation, having to be an overachiever, knowing that it's necessary to be an overachiever, being used, especially in the job sector, where you work very hard knowing that you're going to, or at least thinking that you're going to get a promotion, or get a raise, or just recognition sometimes, and find later that you're not, you're not going to get the recognition, you're not going to get the promotion, the raise. You've just been used. Maybe they'll shift you to another department or maybe out the door even. Oftentimes you're just totally ignored, be it socially, or in the work place. And speaking socially, you have to always be cognizant of the fact that the bulk of White America will never accept you totally, basically because this nation is so race conscious, Black Americans are always fighting a battle with racism. I mean, it is everywhere; it is ingrained in our system.

There are two important issues that this student raises that are outcomes to being marginalized. The first point deals with the very real problem of being overlooked when it comes to promotions and commensurate salary increases. She knows that hard work is required, that it is necessary to be an overachiever even to be in the environment. But, this is most often not enough. Data on wages of White-collar workers indicate that Whites make more and are promoted faster than comparable African American employees. For example, the National Urban League released a study (1990) that compares the relative positions of African Americans to Whites on a number of indices. It shows that it would take 54 years for African Americans to reach parity with Whites in managerial and executive positions. It also indicates that it would take African American males 73 years to close the disparity in the income to Whites.

The second issue that is derived from the comments of this respondent deals with the social psychological impact of being marginalized, which is being in an environment, but not a fully active participant. She says that White people will never fully accept Black people, especially into their social spheres. This statement is only buttressed by the data on attitudes towards interracial marriage, housing segregation, and busing. *A Common Destiny*, (1989) points out that "Blacks are not free to live where they wish, whatever their economic status" (pg. 50).

Another student from the same university describes her feelings of isolation. She notes that most White people don't even recognize how they might be making her feel. She states that:

> I think, well isolation, isolation from people. They don't really include me in things. I don't think they purposely ignore me, you know, I just don't fit the bill, you know. And, I just... when I first came to [the university] I thought the department would really be a wonderful thing because it emphasized how you always had your nice little circle of friends. But none of my major, main friends are in [this department], OK. They stressed how there was such a sense of community, and there isn't any of that. Not in my respect, I didn't feel any of it at all. That's really sad.

This student has experienced what many African Americans experience on a daily basis. She is ignored, considered invisible. Middle class African Americans, often being the only one of the race in an environment, often experience the neglect and loneliness of not having friends from those you deal with so much of your daily life. Again, we see how assimilation and marginality interact. This student is attending a predominately White university and works with the other students in her department. However, as Yetman's (1985) analysis of the assimilation process indicates, these affiliations are secondary institutional alliances, or simply, casual associations. This dynamic suggests that middle-class African Americans are included at the secondary, casual level. But, they are marginalized or kept out of the primary associations and networks. This student, like many other middle class African Americans, is not part of the White community. The superiority/inferiority power relationship is evident in the assimilation process. Marginality provides a vehicle for the dominant society to maintain distance between itself and African Americans.

A seasoned attorney practicing in a large Southwestern city describes the types of situations that send strong messages to African Americans in the work place that they are not wanted. Ostensibly, very minor things, such as not being invited to happy hour gatherings, not being asked to lunches, not receiving guidance or congratulations are all issues that represent barriers to full participation for middle class African Americans. It is more than just the perception of these African Americans. The dynamic interplay of assimilation and marginalization is evident. This attorney is now in private practice in his own law firm:

> Discrimination, insensitivity, you know, I think they're all one and the same. Again, you're one of a few of many. There's not that many of us, be it Black, Hispanic, all women if you add them all together we're not that many. So

you're one of many. And again, for some you're there. We will accept that you're here. For others, but then there's some who don't believe you should be there, so they pretty much won't accept you.

The support that one attorney receives who comes in at the same time as you is different from the support that you receive. It's less. Where you may be in one office and there may be another colleague who came in and is in another office, and a group of attorneys may come up and say, "Jack, let's go and have a drink." And then they walk past your office and say nothing, you know. That's bad. Or let's say that you lose a case. Let's say you both lost a case. Then a partner, a couple of attorneys may come to Jack and say, "Jack, you know, you win some, you lose some. Turn your attention to the other." But, to you, they may say, "What happened? What did you do wrong?" And so, the same sort of encouragement is not there. Either it's discrimination, it's an insensitivity, I could be wrong they're one and the same, you know. So you have to, you're constantly having to deal with that.

The same degree of praise is not there. So there's, I think, though one may not call you, let's say, a "nigger" or may not use derogatory comments, the lack of sensitivity or the lack of support or the lack of praise in a sense does the same. Those things do the same thing.

So it's like sink or swim, you're on your own, and I hope you can do it. So those sort of things you're constantly having to face, and so people wonder why, when you're in corporate America, does it seem like you're isolating yourself from the rest. It's not a matter of YOU isolating yourself, so to speak. It's a matter of being ISOLATED.

This attorney makes clear the conditions of the interaction dynamic of assimilation and marginality. There is the exclusion from primary groups. Many Whites maintain that African Americans are in positions because of legal reasons such as affirmative action programs. So, you are here, but I am not going to support your efforts. There is the lack of support and encouragement. And, this respondent's experience suggests that White people isolate or cut African Americans out of key networks.

African Americans intuitively recognize the "invisible man" syndrome. The plight of the oppressed becomes inconsequential or invisible to the oppressor. Similarly, being in a privileged status desensitizes people to the plight of subordinate groups because they rarely have to see and never have to experience the pain. A professor at a large southwestern university feels as though he is an outcast. This use of this word is important and its use, even more than with 'isolated', indicates the belief among this group of African Americans that being marginalized in this society is a position into which they are placed. The verb used as a noun signifies the active operation of the conscious and unconscious racist behaviors of Whites within the normative structure of the dominant White American ideology.

From my perspective, being Black in America is to be a kind of outcast; to be in something but not of it. For me, quite frankly, I've always thought of myself as a Black man in America. I've probably yet don't think of myself as a Black American, and it's more my resistance, I guess, as clearly as I'm not involved in being very American. But I think for my own personal intimate identity, I see myself as an African American in this country, because I've never felt organically a part of it, despite the geographies that I may have lived in and so forth. So the overall feeling for me is one of being outside, being isolated again, coming of age at some point knowing what it is that this country does in terms of operation of its institutions and its organizations.

A private practice physician in a large eastern urban area views the plight of Blacks in America as second-class citizenry. Even though middle class African Americans have been able to make good money and to attend good schools, this doctor is still isolated and cut off from mainstream society:

Well, I think it's not, I don't find it; you don't feel like you are a part of America. You always feel like you're a second-class citizen. You don't feel like you have, there is the comradeship. You're always isolated. So, from that standpoint, from a social standpoint it's hard. From an economic standpoint, it's good. In my profession, you can go to very good schools and get a very good education. But in terms of being able to interact with society like any other person, it doesn't exist.

## Summary

The assimilation process usually eclipses marginality for most immigrant groups by the second or third generation. Some groups form middleman minorities and emergent ethnic groups through ethnogenesis. African Americans have not been able to follow this same route to inclusion in this society. The marginal status of African Americans has created a strong biculturality—part American and part African and African American. The products of oppression are manifested in the marginal status of African Americans. Isolation, exclusion, feelings of being outcast, of being invisible, and somehow unworthy are a few of the conditions that make up some of the experiences of these respondents and countless other African Americans.

The negative aspects of the marginality of African Americans are profound. Equally present, however, is the oppositional response to these cultural affronts. In the next sections, the biculturality of marginalized middle class African Americans is examined as the cultural creation and response to the oppression of everyday life in White American society.

# Chapter 5
## U.S. Cultural Values

*The American Value System*

Three major components of any culture are language, behavior patterns, and values. Values pose issues dealing with what 'should be' or 'what ought to be'. They are a society's standard of desirability, of rightness, and of importance. Bellah, Madsen, Sullivan, Swidler, and Tipton (1985) open their essay by noting that their book is an engagement about what Americans (White Americans) consider important. They ask their study subjects: "How ought we to live?"(pg. vi) Cultural values determine the norms for a given society and consequently the behavior of its members. The idea of cultural values is useful in focusing on the American core culture and its relation to African Americans.

The important aspect of the dominant White American cultural system is the values that it embodies. As previously stated, the values of a culture inevitably drive behavior. There have been many attempts to delineate the components of an American core culture. Most analysts are able to identify a few components such as individualism, work ethic of hard work leading to success and personal satisfaction, and a few others. I will focus on individualism and strong work ethic.

## *Individualism*

Americans generally believe that individuals have a fundamental responsibility for their own lives, and their successes and failures result from their own efforts and actions. Americans value the right to be in control of their own lives. Herbert Gans (1988) wrote about American individualism as the

> right to be neighborly or to ignore the people next door. It is the ability to be distant from incompatible relatives and to be compatible with friends instead; to skip unwanted memberships in church or union; to vote for candidates not supported by parents or spouses or not to vote at all; and to reject unwelcome advice or demands for behavior change from spouses, employer, or anyone else. (pg. 3)

Max Weber (1958) describes individualism in terms of the Puritan notions of the negativity of emotionality and sensuality. He writes that: "It forms one of the roots of that disillusioned and pessimistically inclined individualism which can even today be identified in the national characters and the institutions of the peoples with a Puritan past..." (Pg. 105). The United States has strong Puritan underpinnings for its founding principles (Franklin and Moss, 1989). English religious tradition was very influential in the forming of American society. The importance of the ascetic Protestantism that many early English settlers brought to the colonies cannot be underestimated. Puritanism was important in establishing the Protestant work ethic at the center of the American value system. (Feagin 1989:69)

Bellah, and his colleagues (1985) point out that there are subtle differences in the traditions of different Americans. However, the motivations for this sense of individualism are tied inextricably to a basic American identity. They write that:

> Individualism lies at the very core of American culture... We believe in the dignity, indeed the sacredness, of the individual. Anything that would violate our right to think for ourselves, judge for ourselves, make our own decisions, live our lives as we see fit, is not only morally wrong, it is sacrilegious. Our highest and noblest aspirations, not only for ourselves, but for those we care about, for our society and for the world, are closely linked to our individualism. (pg. 142)

They continue to suggest that modern individualism emerged out of the struggle against monarchical and aristocratic authority. The issue for this sample of African Americans is different. Scott (1990) describes the cohesion that develops among subordinate groups. He suggests that:

> [M]utual dependence among subordinates favors the development of a distinctive subculture--often one with a strong "us-versus-them" social imagery. Once this occurs, of course, the distinctive subculture itself becomes a powerful force for social unity as all subsequent experiences are mediated by a shared way of looking at the world.

In the struggle against racial oppression, African Americans tend to rely on communal support. For example, a minister explains that when the White world oppresses African Americans, the Black community is there. It does not appear from these comments that African Americans become more individualistic when faced with adversity, as is the route for Whites that is suggested by Bellah, et al. (1985). On the contrary, and closer to Scott's (1989) assessment, it becomes a type of "us against them" dichotomy.

> My family helped me by giving me a strong sense of self-awareness. And my friends the friends that I have, we talk and we're able to process some things and be mutually supportive. But I think that's basically the way I am; I have a strong sense of community. One of the things that we have as Black folk is that when the White world bites us, we know that we can come home and find some healing there. And when I say home, I mean community. A lot of Blacks who have moved out of the Black community have felt alienated and isolated, because they don't have the same kinds of relationships that exist in the social family.

A volunteer worker expresses the sense of security that can only be obtained from contact with the African American community.

> inner security is so important, and being grounded by your own community and friends is important, too, because you know that no matter what happens when you walk out of that room, you go back to an environment that is supportive. And that's very important, I think, for Blacks like myself who are involved in these kinds of environments.

African Americans recognize the value placed on individual achievement this society. However, the common experience of living in a racialized environment of oppression creates a need to be connected to a larger community for support from kindred souls. Staples (1976) explicitly outlines the differences between African and White American values of individualism. He writes that

> White Americans view individualism as each individual making his own mark through competition for the prestige goals of his culture. The rewards of his victory in the competition are his alone. . . . On the other hand, the African American view of the individual is subordinate to a group orientation. It is the group that is important and the Black self is an incorporated part of the social group. Cooperation through collective efforts is the accepted means of achieving culturally prescribed goals. (Staples, 1976:78)

## *Work Ethic*

The belief in a strong work ethic in order to advance successfully in the society is another cultural value the American society holds in reverence. Americans strongly believe in the value of hard work. They believe that hard work leads to business success and personal achievement. The belief in a strong work ethic, says Wallerstein (1983), "is attested by the incorporation within our very superegos of the compulsion to work."(pg. 99) The usual procedure is to get as much education as possible and get a good job. This good job will afford the finer rewards of life in American society. Bellah, et al. (1985) note that work is a critical component for the development of the identity of Americans. They suggest that: "Work continues to be critically important in the self-identity of Americans, closely linked to the demand for self-reliance" (pg. 56).

African Americans share this compulsion for work. Butler (1991) writes about the links between African American entrepreneurship and self help. He suggests that there has been the tradition of entrepreneurship in the African American community. This tradition is exemplified by what he calls the truncated middle class. Differing from the Black bourgeoisie found in Frazier's (1957) classic analysis, the truncated middle class has a tradition from the earliest days of American colonization. African Americans have owned businesses that serviced the broader community as well as the Black community. Butler's thesis suggests that a certain segment of African Americans developed economic stability by maintaining their businesses and crafts. The other strand of African Americans adapted to American society by moving into industry and eventually "created what is called the Afro-American new middle class" (pg. 243). Thusly, the former strand is truncated; or, it has developed a different adaptation to life in America.

The respondents of this study share the same enthusiasm for work and particularly for business ownership. Most of the respondents here are not self-employed. However, many of them have hopes and aspirations for business ownership. It appears that the distinguishing factor between African American work ethic and White American work ethic is to be found in the motivations. For White Americans work is a means to individual achievement. For example, Weber (1958) has noted that the work ethic is directly attributable to Puritanism. He writes that there was applause from

> a believing world, in expressing the emotions of the faithful Puritan, thinking only of his own salvation. It is expressed in the unctuous conversations which he holds with fellow-seekers on the way... Only when he himself is safe does it occur to him that it would be nice to have his family with him. (pg. 107)

More directly attributable to American styled individualism and work ethic is the assessment by Bellah et al. (1985). They note from an analysis of Ralph Waldo Emerson's (1841) essay *Self-reliance* that:

> Emerson also expressed a more prosaic sense of self-reliance, one that has been the common coin of moral life for millions of Americans ever since. Emerson says that we only deserve the property we work for. Conversely, our primary economic obligation is only to ourselves... We found self-reliance common as a general orientation in many of those to whom we spoke. (pg. 56)

A more common experience that is related from the respondents of this study suggests that they are more concerned with community. The work ethic for African Americans is one of developing the Black community. As suggested earlier, this may be borne out of the oppression that subordinate groups experience in the society (Scott, 1990). In other words, oppressed groups do not have the luxury of selfishness. The entire community is needed to survive the oppression that is experienced. "Successful" Blacks, as most of the respondents here call themselves, have a definite need to give back to the community. A nursing professor recognizes that she was not always successful and that she did not get successful without help. She urges a strong commitment to the community from successful African Americans.

> One of the things as a "successful" Black is that I wasn't always successful. Now from my early upbringing, I guess I could always be classified as middle class. So could my husband. However, within my early years in association as a child in a segregated community of all African Americans economically maybe a few people were put on a pedestal, but for the most part everybody was at the same level, struggling Black Americans. Now, the situation is when

you get reasonably successful, then you have to give something back to the community, and you have to make a commitment to that.

Commonly experienced oppression creates a type of solidarity among individuals. This solidarity is supported by reliance on the community of the oppressed. African Americans, as stated by the above respondent, are all struggling. A strong work ethic is part of the struggle to survive; but the survival is of a community not just the individual.

These cultural values of individualism and strong work ethic are reified and embodied in the ideology of American culture. It is suggested that cultural values dictate what the norms and behavior patterns for the members of a given society "should be" or "ought to be". Language, through its symbolism, conveys and reinforces a society's ideological worldview.

## *The American Core Culture as the Standard*

These values became reified in the ideals of democracy. Notions of freedom, justice, and equality of opportunity are the operationalizations of American styled democracy. Colonial efforts created an anglicized version of these ideals and Anglo conformity was accepted as the way to full inclusion in American society (McLemore, 1991). We can conclude from this reasoning that these concepts became more than just components of the culture. In reified form they became the very "standards against which any other group's location and progress could be measured"(McLemore, 1991:44).

To be fully incorporated as American, then, groups must embrace these ideals as their own culture. Any group that does not share the same fervor and commitment to these values is viewed as an outsider and treated with utter disdain. Much more was the case of African Americans. Because of racism, African Americans are barred from full participation in American society even though they fully embrace the standards of the culture.

This distinctive situation of African Americans makes an Afrocentric study of this aspect of their life experience of critical importance to a broader understanding of that experience. In the following section, I introduce the idea of middle class African American biculturality. It involves knowing the intricacies of the culture of the oppressor and using the African American culture as an agent of resistance and change.

## *U.S. Value System: Afrocentric Biculturality*

African Americans own a unique history in the American experience. Africans were brought to this nation in chains as labor to build the profits of imperialist colonizers. The subsequent 370 years of slavery, segregation, and continuing racism and discrimination have necessitated equally creative responses to these life conditions.

African Americans had to learn White culture in order to survive. Blauner (1972) points out that there are "pressures of White institutions to remake Afro-Americans in those middle class [White] ways that acceptance and success seem to require"(pg. 145). In order to survive, African Americans at all class levels have had to become adept at White ways of doing. The African American middle class that spends considerable time in the "White world" feels this pressure even more. There is always the pressure to conform or to give up a part of one's Afro-American self. The middle class African American is placed in a dilemma. Du Bois (1946) suggests that the middle class African American is likely to be in a heretofore "lily-White" environment and "may meet peculiar frustration and in the end be unable to achieve success in the new environment or fit into the old [African American community]" (pg. 144). Du Bois seems to be suggesting here also that a careful balance must be struck in order to avoid being left in a limbo state or in a cultural void.

## *Knowing "White" American Culture*

Knowing White American culture for African Americans means having a deep understanding of the intricacies of the culture; it means, "being" White. Middle class African Americans find it especially important to be an expert at "Whiteness". The manager of a large electronics company in the southwest pointedly talks about having to "lose your identity" and become White in order to be successful. He says that:

> If you're going to be successful, you almost lose your identity as a Black person totally, your culture, the things you're comfortable with, in order to at least get work done. Because most of the time you're working in any environment, a business environment, you almost transform from doing the things you're comfortable with to the things you've learned to do, in order to be successful.

This successful businessman is specific in his description of putting aside the Black culture that, to him, is an uncomfortable thing to do. It is a transformation that African Americans have learned to do well to be successful in this society. He also recognizes that most of the settings in which he might find himself are going to be White; so, he knows how to act in these situations. He knows that many decisions are made outside the office and to be successful you have to be where those decisions are being made.

> Most business is transacted in a social setting. And that social setting is always going to be in a White social setting, not a Black social setting. If you're going to work with your managers and your upper managers, that's never in a Black environment, that's always in a White environment. In order to fit in it is important not to appear threatening to White people.

Certain African American idiomatic forms may be considered threatening by Whites such as Black slang and other dialectical forms, music types, and modes of dress. White stereotypes of African Americans inform much of this attitude. In knowing White culture, African Americans must know that this evaluation of them is deeply ingrained through years of continuing racialized socialization and try to use it to their advantage. Fitting in implies merging into the existing format or program. To be accepted, African Americans must not appear threatening to White people. Notice how this respondent speaks of the image of the African American in the White mind. Whites see the "Black" skin, which triggers long reinforced negative images—inferior, drug addict, sexual deviate and hypersexuality, rapist, murderer, robber, and the stereotypes go on. These misconceptions are all traceable to the inability of African Americans to assimilate into the so-called mainstream.

> So, in order for you to at least fit, you have to not, not be Black, in order for them not to be intimidated by you. Because their image of a Black person is inferior, and that's the tape they played and learned over the years. So, you almost have to lose some of those threatening things that you know that they feel uncomfortable with in order for you just to talk with them one on one, in a normal environment.

Doing things that may not be exciting or interesting to you is part of this game. The stereotype is that African Americans are best suited for heavy contact sports or activities that do not require much strategy or patience to accomplish. But, for middle class African Americans, knowing that this attitude exists prepares this respondent to meet this challenge and go on to destroy this stereotype. For instance, if he has to play golf, he learned how to do it.

> I don't feel uncomfortable in social settings, if they want to go play golf, I'll go play golf with them. If they have a party at their house, I could go there and laugh and talk and joke and jive. And at the same time I still have a Black side of me that I know, that this is part of the game, and this is my life over here. And my Black side is my life.

This respondent separates the game that is played with White people from his life. He recognizes his duality. Playing the game is maintaining a balance. And, the successful balancing act recognizes that life is being Black. The components outlined in the preceding excerpt are important and recurring variables in knowing White culture. This is an important factor in the biculturality of African Americans. Playing the game, submerging Black identity, transforming cultures—Black into White, fitting in by dropping characteristics perceived as threatening by Whites, recognizing the stereotypes, and the duality of roles will be seen as ever-present themes with many of the respondents of this study. Middle class African Americans understand the importance of knowing White culture.

Let us examine how another respondent describes the idea of "knowing White culture". This student is attending a major southwestern university. He does not have the experience of the previous respondent, being only twenty-two years old; but he is able to articulate the same wisdom about knowing White culture. Even at this young age, this student knows that in order to be successful: "you have to get them to like you in spite of you being Black, I think. You know, he's Black but he's ok. That's the sort of syndrome you could fall into."

This student also knows about putting on a facade. African Americans must "hold down" their "Blackness" as not to make White folks nervous.

> I don't think most people are consciously aware that they have to be superficial, but toward the end, I guess, if you really think about it, I guess you'd have to be to an extent, so not have to worry about upsetting them, or making them nervous, because you're being super into your Black things. Because other people don't like to, you know, oh, he's being too ethnic. So, you just keep on a level where everything's pretty much on the surface, you don't have to delve into the personal characteristics, and you can get along easier I think.

This young respondent makes an interesting insight. He mentions the plasticity of Black people, the requirement that African Americans must fit into a White mold. And just as with the electronics manager, African Americans do things they may prefer not to do.

> And most of the time Black people have to be almost plastic in their own personal opinions just to go with the opinions of most White folks, just to get along, to do certain things, like going to movies, or just listening to bands. If you're with a large group of Whites and there's a small number of Blacks, you pretty much will get out voted on where to go, you pretty much pretend, or will put up with it just to go with the evening, when you'd rather be someplace listening to real good jazz, or whatever, a Black oriented music place.

And, again, the submerging of Black identity in order to get ahead is prominent in this respondent's remarks. He recognizes the duality of being African American, mentioning that home is the only place to really be Black. He laments this tragic condition of Black life in White America and resolves that African Americans will continue to suffer with the system if they want to achieve any modicum of success.

> So, I think most Black people have to hold back the stuff that they really like, the stuff that would identify and make them Black, just so they can be accepted and get along and work with the White people, since they're going to have to be in a [White] situation a majority of the time. I guess when they come home, is when they really become, when they're really Black, and it's just a shame, because they have to hold that back when around White people... So, Black people will just have to suffer for a while and just work with that, it's a system they have to work with if they want to get anything.

Today, for African Americans, "knowing White culture" involves more than just having to learn the "correct" or "proper" English language. It involves knowing and understanding White American values and subsequent behavioral roles or ways of conduct in the society. Middle class African Americans, particularly, spend a large amount of time interacting with White people. In order to achieve the goals they have set for themselves and their families, these middle class African Americans adopt a strategy that will "get them past" White insecurities and prejudices. Getting past these formidable barriers is a task that consumes much energy and effort from these African Americans.

African Americans through 370 years of intimate contact with the dominant White culture have an equally intimate understanding of White culture. Middle class African Americans embrace the values of individualism, and strong work ethic. They strive toward these ideals. But, the motivation, constraints, and goals differ from the total assimilative nature demanded by the articulation of these factors by the dominant White American culture. In the next section, I explore African American culture as it responds to the differing motivations, constraints, and goals of life in White American society.

## *African Heritage-American Culture*

The African American culture is a complex phenomenon to define. It is composed of at least two major components--African and American. However, it is more than just a concept. For, like all cultures, it is not static. It is forever changing. It is adapting—being pushed and pulled and at the same time pushing and pulling within a mix of other cultures and particularly the American core culture. It was stated previously that the unique experience of African Americans in this society calls for equally unique responses. Levine (1977) concurs in that the toughness and resiliency of a culture are not determined by its ability to withstand change, but by its ability to react creatively and responsively to the realities of a new situation. African American culture provides an interesting study of the way a culture of oppressed people responds to domination by another culture. In this section I will outline the basic constituents of African American culture. The voices of African American experiences will show how this culture pushes its agenda while at the same time being sensitive to the demands of the dominant core culture of American society.

## *African Retentions*

African American culture is both African and American. The American traits are recognizable in such things as language forms, types of foods consumed, and basic religious worship structure. The "American-ness" of African Americans seems little in question. However, there has been and continues to be quite some debate about the remnants of a type of "Africanness" to be found in the culture of Americans of African heritage. Where there is no question of African retentions in African American culture, the issue of degrees arises. That is, how much African can be found; and, is it the same across socio-economic levels?

African Americans have been here for nearly 400 years. Brought here as slaves for the most part, there were flagrant attempts to "deculturate" them. In order to insure against organized rebellion, or anything approaching defiance, slave families were separated and members of the same communities were dispersed. However, Franklin and Moss (1989) indicate, "at least some survival of African culture is obvious"(pg. 26).

Earlier, the core White, Anglo-Saxon, protestant dominant core culture was discussed. It was stated that this model is the pattern to which everyone wishing to be "American" had to conform. Hence, the term Anglo conformity is produced. African Americans were put into a position of forced assimilation. Slaves were forced to learn the master's language in order to perform their duties. Of course, failure in this area meant harsh punishment and possibly death.

Throughout the long history of African American and White American interaction, African Americans have learned the White culture well. Because African Americans learned this alternative culture so well, some analysts, such as E. Franklin Frazier and Robert Park conclude that there is no evidence of anything in the modern African American that can be traced to an African background. This supposition, for some scholars, finds validity in the belief that United States slavery eroded the language forms and the institutional side of African life and, therefore, wiped out almost all of the fundamental aspects of traditional African culture. For example, Robert Park (1919) writes that

> the Negro, when he landed in the United States, left behind him almost everything but his dark complexion and his tropical temperament.... Coming from all parts of Africa and having no common language and common tradition, the memories of Africa which they brought with them were soon lost.

Following these earlier analysts, Gordon (1964) tries to support his assimilationist views of African Americans when he asserts that:

> Few African cultural survivals are to be found among American Negroes. Middle and upper class Negroes, on the other hand, are acculturated to American core culture. (pg. 76)

This position fails to consider the fact that language and social institutions alone do not embrace the fullness of culture. It cannot be disputed that Africans forced to the United States as slaves had to give up many of the structural aspects of their native cultures. However, much of the foundations remained intact. Further, most, if not all of the worldviews remained and, arguably flourished. Franklin and Moss (1989) point out that African slaves came from a complex civilization and were not awe struck by the experiences of colonial America. And further, they state that there were at least two acculturative processes going on side by side in the New World. As Africans of different experiences live together, there was the interaction of the various African cultures. These produced a somewhat different set of customs and practices, but these were still manifestly rooted deep in the African experience. (Franklin and Moss, 1989:26)

To be sure, these processes were not, and are not mutually exclusive. Again it is an ongoing interaction of cultures that recreates, unique adaptations to the social situation. The essence of African American culture can be found in the creative and responsive transformations dictated by the experience of oppression in this society. Roger Bastide (1971) makes clear this specific point. Paraphrasing his argument, he posits that in order to survive a given situation, a people adapt the culture. Hence, the form remains African and the transformation becomes the expression. It is suggested that this expression is a combined transformation of the dominant culture and retentions of African cultures that are now uniquely African American.

The issue is simplified to what degree are middle-class African Americans aware of their African cultural background? Does this awareness inform their worldviews in anyway? And, of course, how do they see the interplay of their "African-ness" with their "American-ness"? Most of the respondents in this sample have an acute awareness of their African heritage. The interesting factor is how they see the interplay of their duality of cultures.

The following respondent recognizes the influence of his "African-ness" in shaping his understanding of himself and the world. He views this heightened awareness of his African heritage as a definite positive for attaining success in American society today. His outlook about success is

> very confident. One thing about coming into consciousness or learning about African heritage is that you realize how spiritual a people we are; I was always brought up in the church, but this search of mine to seek and find as much African knowledge as possible has really made me a much more spiritual person, and with that in me, I know that whatever I want to do, I can do. I honestly believe I can do anything.

Seeking knowledge of African heritage is a key to success. The following conversation demonstrates the importance of knowing your roots.

> I try to stress to them not only knowing math and knowing science, but knowing your African roots. You know, knowing your roots here in America as well as knowing your African roots. I mean that's the only way we're going to be able to get over this self-doubt.

This respondent discusses that one of the consequences of being in a perpetual state of marginalization is self-doubt. As it was previously discussed, being kept on the outside, just on the fringes produces a type of inferiority complex. One begins to wonder whether, or not it is actually innate inability that thwarts attempts to be successful. This respondent sees knowledge of African and American heritages as the only way to guard against these feelings of self-doubt. Likewise, a college professor at a major southern university sees a movement away from the African heritage and traditional focus on the family/community unit. She believes that: "It's an issue where, as African Americans, we've moved away from our heritage, we've moved away from the family unit that made us strong."She sees this loss as a result of the encroachment of American styled individualism into African American institutions such as the church.

> And the other thing is the change in the African American church. Church used to be the basis, or the home base, where we got our nurturing, our growth and development of our self-esteem, where our political base started and ended in the '60s and the '70s. In the '90s there's so much self promotion within the African American church that it's kind of lost sight of its goals.

This professor is well aware of being in a White environment most of the time. She and her family live in a predominantly White neighborhood and teaches at a predominantly White university. In order to resist the imposition of the dominant White American culture, which she views as not totally beneficial to African Americans, she states that African Americans must be solidly grounded in their heritage and must teach it to the children. Middle class African Americans, in particular, need to be sensitive to the need to remain connected with the greater masses. African Americans, particularly the middle class, must remain in touch with the community that established them; it will also maintain them.

> Consequently, living where we live, apart from the predominantly African American community, we have to put forth an effort to make sure that we get this child across town to activities that would allow him a certain amount of socialization with African American children. We do this through his participation in the YMCA on the east side of [the city], which is predominantly African American; through church activities, like the church choir; family outings through the church that, in our particular church, we go on a regular basis. As far as our own socialization and social life is concerned, we primarily are friends with other professionals and we go outside of our area in order to socialize.

It is very important to these middle class African Americans that both African and African American heritages be taught. The implicit knowledge from these experiences ensures that African Americans will continue to improve their condition.

> One of the things is we have to go back and take a look at our history. We have to make sure that our children see our history. Now, as a kid growing up in Black schools, Black history was very much a part of my education. NOT what the history book had to tell me. Should I believe that, then I can also say that I'm going to win the lottery tomorrow. Not what I was told by those teachers, but what I was taught in my home. And one of the things we do in our home is we have African American calendars. And every day on those calendars something happened that affected Black people, African people, or a mixture of both. The history that is taught cannot be the history that is in the books in school.

This respondent sees the importance of sharing the experiences of African Americans from that unique perspective. Utilizing the strong institutions in the community, like the church, to impress upon the youth the value of our people and the contributions that Africans and African Americans have made to the world community.

A young minister expresses the importance of understanding that African in front of American is critical to survival in this society. He implores African Americans to develop a sense of identity based on the unique experiences of life in the United States, building on the long, rich history of Africans and African Americans.

> First of all, they're gonna have to develop a sense of history from their own perspective. You know, we are taught basically from four hundred years ago to present, and when Blacks talk about themselves, they start their history saying he's an American. And we can't do that, we can't do that. We have to go further than that, and see the great African kings and great kingdoms and the great contributions that we as a people have made to civilization.... Because if you take a book that's written by a White Anglo-Saxon, you're gonna get his perspective. And his perspective is tainted. So we're going to have to expand our minds by being able to expose ourselves to different thoughts and ideas, and particularly from the Afro American perspective.

A graduate student who works with youth in an urban community center describes the importance of understanding the African American experience and recognizing the African heritage in that experience.

> I think to really understand what it is to be Black in America you really have to have an appreciation for Black culture, you have to understand Black culture, which I guess is African American culture. And you have to have some knowledge of your heritage, which involves possessing some knowledge about Africa and I guess more importantly about the Black experience here in America. I mean those are the things you have to think about, the things that you have to be cognizant of constantly.

This articulate student sees the African and African American heritages as the foundation for building strong communities and institutions: "Those are the things that give you the urge to develop the strong Black communities, to raise your consciousness, to make you realize the need to develop strong Black institutions, and strong Black communities."He further sees the development of these strong African American institutions as important because of barriers erected that prevent full participation in mainstream institutions. He recognizes that African Americans can never

> Fully integrate into a society that is unwilling to appreciate or respect who you are and what you stand for. And America yet is sort of a young country, the racist history that still exists today. It's still just a dominant theme of this society. Being Black encompasses realizing all of that and that, this sense of identity, I mean, this sense of pride, not getting caught up in mainstream America.

And, finally, this young respondent expounds on the frustrating struggle to be at peace with oneself. He has learned the struggle of being African American. The struggle is overcome by seeking more knowledge and a deeper understanding of African heritage and its transformation into African American culture.

> When I began to understand my history, and what my history included and my history being African American history, what it was about, you know, the ups and downs, the struggles, the ideological perspectives, just all the different angles, I don't guess this is conclusive, I think I'm developing a strong Black mind and a strong Black identity. I feel at peace with myself. And by that I mean, I feel as though I'm just as capable as anybody else, be they White, Black, red or brown. I don't have that obstacle to worry with.

> But it's like the more you become aware of our history, and the more you become aware of things you've never even considered, things that you weren't taught in school, things that were seemingly kept from you, it's frustrating. There's this constant struggle to gain more knowledge to gain a stronger, and more complete historical perspective. For me personally, the most important factor is to accept myself, appreciate who I am, what I stand for, and have a full understanding of all the struggles that have been made that now allow me to do some of the things that I'm able to do, lives that have been lost.

> And I think that those things go beyond mere rhetoric and those are some sincere feelings that you have to come to grips with. You can appreciate who you are, once you can accept the fact of who you are, an African American, is just as good as anybody else in this world, psychologically that equips you with the necessary tools to go out and be competitive.

These few examples demonstrate the importance middle class African Americans place on their African heritage that, in part, created African American culture. They clearly understand the interaction of White American core culture with African culture.

## Summary

African American culture has been formed through the intimate interacting of centuries of Africanized and Americanized cultural traditions. The values which support the traditions of White American culture form a central organizing principle for this chapter. The traditions of democracy, justice, and equality of oppor-tunity are supported by ideological values such as individualism and strong work ethic. The data herein have suggested that these same values have been adopted by many of the middle class African American respondents. However, what is evident is that the means-end relationship or motivation is different from that of White Americans. African Americans value individualism and hard work as the means toward the result of strengthening and improving the African American community, not primarily for individualistic gain.

Consistent with the marginality experienced by these respondents, African Americans, out of necessity, are bicultural. In order to survive, they must have a thorough knowledge of the dominant White culture. Coping with the stories of heavy oppression these respondents recount, they rely on the foundation of the African American culture and community. Middle class African Americans are caught in a particularly sensitive position. They spend a great deal of time having to interact with Whites. Therefore, middle class African Americans must know White American traditions, customs, and behaviors.

The transformations of the Africanisms into the utility of an African American culture are, at once, creative and reactive. It is creative in the sense that a uniquely African American culture is evolving and changing the White American culture. And, it is reactive in the sense that part of the African American culture is in response to the oppressive nature of life in the dominant American society. It is to this cultural response to oppression in America that attention is directed.

# Chapter 6
## Cultural Opposition

*Oppositional Culture*

The idea of cultural opposition was foreshadowed in the work of Du Bois (1903). In discussing his opposition to the general accommodationist position of Booker T. Washington, Du Bois wrote that:

> Newly freed African Americans, as the imprisoned group, may take on three main forms, a feeling of revolt and revenge; an attempt to adjust all thought and action to the will of the greater group; or finally, a determined effort at self-realization and self-development despite environing opinion. (DuBois, 1903:243-244)

In an article published in 1960, Du Bois argues strongly against assimilation on the grounds that it would mean cultural extinction. He writes that:

> What I have been fighting for and am still fighting for is the possibility of Black folk and their cultural patterns existing in America without discrimination; and on terms of equality... We must also lay down a line of thought and action which will accomplish two things: The utter disappearance of color discrimination in American life and the preservation of African history and culture as a valuable contribution to modern civilization. (DuBois, 1960:150-151)

Although DuBois did not explicitly outline the dimensions of a notion of cultural opposition, his ideas form the basic or germinal thoughts on an oppositional culture of African Americans.

Further work on the idea of oppositional culture has been forwarded by Michael Hechter (1975) with his study of the English colonization of the Irish. This colonialism approach suggests that before colonizers occupy the land, there are indigenous groups that have in place functional cultures and societies. When these groups of people are colonized, their cultures are not destroyed. On the contrary, the indigenous culture resists, in various ways, domination (Scott, 1990). Victimized groups of neo-colonialism, such as African Americans, draw on their own cultural resources, such as extended kinship ties, strong beliefs in ideals of justice and democracy to resist cultural, as well as, physical domination.

The African American response to oppressive regimes of racism and discrimination in American society is one of continuing struggle. The changing face of modern American racism belies its insidious nature and the dire consequences to its African American targets in all social and economic realms.

Consequently, they remain engaged on many levels in a continuing battle for legitimacy in an environment that is at opposition to these very efforts. W.E.B. DuBois (1975) contended that there is a war between the races and that this is the dominant theme of the twentieth century. He wrote that: "we are planning not peace but war [against] the continued oligarchical control of civilization by the White race (p. v.)." Samuel F. Yette (1971) concurs with philosophical support from John Locke that "the racial factor has counted even more heavily in the country's domestic wars than in the international sphere. . . . America, certainly since bringing slaves to these shores in 1619, has been in a perpetual state of war"(pg. 75).

Dubois wrote in *Black Reconstruction* about the imperative of African American entry into the "mainstream" society. There can be no compromise of self or culture. He says that it must be on terms of indisputable equality. In the struggle to be on equal standing with their White counterparts, African Americans know that they are in a battle for cultural and physical survival. DuBois' words cut directly to the heart of the issue when he writes:

> This the American Black man knows: his fight here is a fight to the finish. Either he dies or wins. If he wins, it will be by no subterfuge or evasion of amalgamation. He will enter modern civilization here in America a Black man on terms of perfect and unlimited equality with any White man, or he will enter not at all. Either extermination root and branch, or absolute equality. There can be no compromise. This is the last great battle of the West. (DuBois, *Black Reconstruction*, pg. 703)

African Americans have known that they have been in a battle for survival since arriving in chains in Jamestown, VA in 1619. The battle lines were definitively drawn when the first group of Africans was enslaved in the New World. The veiled attempts to strip the native culture from African slaves were met with various forms of resistance. Slaves killed owners and overseers, burned plantations, performed work slowdowns and even work stoppages (strikes). More than this type of opposition, African Americans transformed African and American traits into a useful and forceful response to White American cultural hegemony.

In the following section, the narratives of the respondents are used to show that there is a keen understanding of the power relationship between White and African American cultures. Many of the respondents subscribe to what has been called the "Black Power Imperative."

## *Black Power: Assertion of Black Culture*

The idea of Black power is not new. Marcus Garvey was probably the first to coin it in the 1920s and Richard Wright wrote a book of that title in 1954. It was thrown into the racial struggle more directly when it was used as the rallying call of the Student Nonviolent Coordinating Committee (SNCC) in the mid 1960s. The words conjure up images of African American men with the right arm held high overhead with tightly clenched fists. This allegory symbolizes the opposition to an oppression that has required its victims to lie flat and non-expressive. The vertical extension of a powerful fist symbolizes the resurrection of a people whose culture has been buried by centuries of assault.

The concept of Black Power, in all its complexity, is a call for African Americans to use group or community solidarity for survival. Hamilton (1969) has identified seven meanings of Black Power. First Black Power means Black consciousness. This component involves the emphasis of race pride, African and African American culture, history, and heritage. Secondly, there is an undercurrent of hatred towards White people. Third, there is the component of violence. This violence can be viewed as two types—expressive and instrumental. Expressive violence typically takes the form of random, indiscriminate rioting and looting. Instrumental violence, on the other hand, is directed and highly disciplined towards targets that are picked carefully with specific and strategic goals as the focus. The embodiment of this type of violence can become a support and rallying system in the community.

A fourth component of Black Power takes the form of separatism. Proponents of this idea suggest establishing a separate Black nation. Most of the "back to Africa" separatists have fallen out of prominence; but there is some advocacy for establishing such a nation from existing states within this country. Black capitalism is another facet that emphasizes African American business entrepreneurship and ownership. It focuses on capital that is invested and used in and for the African American community. A closely related aspect is that of community control. And, finally, the seventh meaning of Black Power is that of political pressure. Political power is to be gained through the support and election of African Americans.

These components mix interactively and dynamically within the African American community. They change, in varying degrees, to fit the needs of the community. An example is the aftermath of the Rodney King travesty. Rodney King, a young African American in the Los Angeles area was stopped for speeding and the ensuing encounter lead to several police officers brutally beating the motorist. The possibility of this type of treatment from law enforcement officials is a constant fear of African Americans from all class levels (see Feagin, 1991). This beating was captured on videotape and it was thrown into the national headlines. The officers were brought to trial and acquitted of the brutality charges. It seems to me that the uprising was legitimate in the context of Black Power. The evidence indicates that violence had been heaped upon the African American community and the proverbial "straw" was the senseless and unjustifiable beating of Mr. King. Now, whether the violence was expressive or instrumental awaits further analysis.

The focus here will be on issues of Black consciousness, Blacks' distrust of Whites, and Black capitalism. These components of the Black Power paradigm embody the thrust of middle class African American resistance to White cultural hegemony.

## Black Consciousness

It was mentioned in the previous section that White American culture is the dominant factor in this society. This dominant culture becomes the standard by which all else is evaluated. There are many ways in which the hegemony of White American culture is translated and communicated. The images that are portrayed to us via various print and electronic media aid in this socialization process. The images that are seen are not only reflections of the dominant hegemony they are strong indoctrination forces. These forces are communicated as the ideal to achieve. For African Americans the images are the same; however, they rarely include African American values.

Examples can be seen in the images on television. The things and values that are rewarded are those deemed appropriate and worthy by those of the dominant White American culture. This message is communicated to everyone in the society over and over. Hollywood is not the only progenitor of the dominant hegemony. It is common to see television advertisements for religious crusade organizations where they use footage from previous services. These footages do not feature anything remotely resembling the general African American worship or religious experience. So, hegemony manifests itself not only in the superficiality of some entertainment ethic; but it also springs forth from the deepest held values of the society, such as religion.

These concerns, which probably seem innocuous to most White Americans, erode the value of the identity of any of the subordinate groups in the society. The over-riding aim is, of course, Anglo conformity. If success in the society is desired, then subordinate groups must assimilate into the dominant group by taking on the dominant group's culture.

However, African Americans face the barrier of race, or as DuBois (1903) put it, the "problem of the color line." African Americans are prevented from following the standard route of assimilation and integration (Gordon, 1964), and in response, they have created a uniquely African American culture in order to resist the onslaught of the dominant White American culture.

The African American middle class is not retreating from the onslaught of the White American core culture. The transformations developed to oppose this assault can be seen in the ongoing development of Black consciousness. A self-employed political analyst in a large Southwestern city sees Whites as keeping African Americans unbalanced. In order to counter this and have a solid foundation on which to hold, African Americans must think based on an Afrocentric world view. She says that it is important that: "we learn how to develop our own Black consciousness. See, the brothers and sisters get trapped because they're not thinking for themselves." This respondent's experience is evidence of the imperative of developing a sense of ownership of African American heritage. Knowing Black history is important in avoiding the traps of ignorance.

Black consciousness recognizes the costs of emulating Whites. Black Power is the direct ideological and cultural opposition to the notion of Anglo conformity (White power) expectations of White culture. This articulate spokeswoman shares the essence of the cultural resistance of African Americans.

> You see to develop Black consciousness is to say to America, "America, we will no longer emulate you; and you, America, will no longer violate the existence of our culture. For you see, I refuse to be confused." That's important. This is important for us. To develop Black consciousness is to be able to confront, challenge, and denounce a demented system that carries with it justice for some but not justice for all.

Like many of the other respondents, for this entrepreneur developing Black consciousness is liberating. It is taking a stand for true freedom within this society by liberating the African American mind from the conditioning of White society. She says that to develop Black consciousness is to

> rip those shackles off of your feet, to erase this conditioning from your mind, and to begin a debriefing process. That's what that's all about. Cause, now, if that person is debriefed, then they can understand, it ain't important what they [Whites] think.

This respondent illustrates the critical importance for African Americans to develop their own sense of identity and no longer just copy what White America is doing, for this is a way that they are trapped by the system. Black consciousness, for this respondent, means getting rid of the ideas that have been so long socialized into African Americans. She says that African Americans must begin debriefing themselves.

It was aforementioned that stereotyping is used by the dominant culture to reassert its authority over subordinate groups. It is important to resist the stereotypes that are used to suppress and denigrate African Americans by the dominant culture. A graduate student at a Southwestern university explains the importance of knowing who you are as an African American.

> At some point in time if you don't realize that you are Black and that you have a unique history in this country, you're going to have real problems. I think just in order to feel full as a person, and in their case as a young man, they're going to have to accept and appreciate and be proud of who they are. And it goes beyond, far beyond just the regular 'I'm Black and I'm proud', I mean you have to fully appreciate who you are, and be proud of who you are. And realize that just because you're Black doesn't mean in order to be perceived as a good student you have to go out and act what has been defined as the proper way which is often times associated with being White.

Coming to grips with this reality is important because to believe that emulating White culture will make you more acceptable is a myth. It was previously suggested that the process of assimilation and popular ideas about the United States as a melting pot or as God's crucible do not explain the experience lived by African Americans in this society. At the same time, it is critical to understand that African Americans are as socialized by these ideals and values as is anyone in this society.

African Americans deeply embrace the ideals of freedom, equality, and democracy. One respondent says "I really believed in integration, in the idea of us all coming together as one, as American."But, the sentiment of DuBois' (1903) statement that the "problem of the twentieth century is the problem of the color line" is true because African Americans were never in the plans for incorporation and therefore the assimilation process is not valid as the mobility trek for them. This student echoes DuBois when he reveals the reality that sooner or later White America will block any attempts by African Americans to be fully included.

## Distrust of Whites

Hamilton (1969) wrote that one of the meanings or components of Black Power is a hatred of Whites. Many of the respondents in the present study describe their experiences with Whites that lead them to articulate an instinctive distrust for White people. To ascribe feelings or sentiments of hatred may go beyond the descriptions given. However, the reader does not get the feeling of abiding faith and love from the respondents' words used to describe their experiences with White people. There is a definite suspicion of the underlying motivations of Whites. The White power establishment of this country has made many promises. Most of these assurances have not been carried out. Historical examples ranging from forty acres and a mule, to the "promise" of integration have never come to fruition.

The respondents in this study, while aware of these "grand" promises, distrust Whites because of their everyday dealings with them. These powerful statements are real experiences, not some lofty theory about a situation. They raise the serious question of what have Whites done to be experienced by middle class African Americans this way? African Americans have done all the things deemed necessary along the road to ultimate assimilation, and hence, successes, only to have the floor fall from them. They have seen and felt the sabotage, exclusion, and the everyday racism of White people.

The negative experiences that these respondents recount are supported by the perception of White Americans the world over. White supremacy stretches across the world and engulfs everyone in its oppressive snare. Quoting from *The Autobiography of Malcolm X*, Manning Marable (1984:97) writes that the White man's "evil and his greed cause him to be hated around the world." The far-reaching impact of American styled White supremacy is demonstrated in a cross-cultural study by Philomena Essed (1990, 1991). She conducted a comparative analysis of the racism and discrimination experienced by Black

Surinamese-Dutch and African American women. In this study, Essed (1990) found the contours of racism and discrimination to be very similar between both societies, being "based on the same ideology of White superiority."(pg. 258) She further concludes that distrust is part of experiencing everyday racism. "It means being ever-alert to exactly what is going on during one's contact with Whites... It causes people of color to anticipate racism in their contact with Whites..." (pg. 259).

Similarly, a college sophomore who felt that an elder was being overly bitter towards White people when she warned her not to trust White people learned the harsh reality of everyday dealings with Whites.

> I don't think I'll ever really trust most White people... most Whites I wouldn't trust. Just from my roommate experience, that really got me. Like during my senior year, my aunt told me, don't trust White people, they will stab you in the back, they will talk about you. And I said, no, you don't know what you're talking about, you're just bitter. And then it just turns around and happens to me.

A self-employed business consultant in a medium sized Southwestern city explains her distrust of Whites, especially White liberals.

> Even, and especially those so called liberals, I absolutely have no respect for them. I do not trust them. Because see they'll befriend you, they've got to have their Black friends to show how liberal they are, and they understand the cause, and they understand shit, because they ain't been through it. And they want to tell you about self determination, as long as they can sit there and determine what self determination should be for you, they're fine.

> But the day you question them, or say I don't agree with it, then you can kind of see that little friendship on the wane. And they have a limitation on how far they'll go with you. As long as they're all massed up together with their little liberals, then everything is fine. But when it's isolated and they really have to prove their little liberalism and their little affirmative bullshit, well, then they'll tell you, well, John or Mary, this is as far as I can go. You know, I know you're right, but see if I do that, I may lose my job, or I may lose this. So, they wake up in the morning just as conservative as any conservative person.

This respondent is blunt in her assessments. She views Whites as using rhetoric, such as self-determination, to impose their ways of doing or their belief system on African Americans. Whites will always assert their agenda and its desirability over any other program or position. She contends that even though Whites may come off as being friends, as soon as you disagree on an issue that scratches the thin membrane of liberalism; they begin to recoil into dominant core ways of relating and behaving.

It is often said that trust is not given but must be earned. The position of this respondent, and others, is very understandable. The historical treatment of

74 Cultural Opposition

African Americans by the White dominant culture does not bode well for establishing trust. This entrepreneur must deal with Whites everyday in her consulting practice. And, her success is, in part, tied to her understanding of the "back-stabbing" treatment of African Americans by White Americans. In an upbraiding report, she focuses on the motivations of White folks in dealing with African Americans. She indicates that behind the liberalism White racism is influencing the motivations of Whites. The racist stereotypes of African American culture are deeply socialized into the psyche of most Whites, even so-called liberals.

> So, I don't trust them. I don't trust them at all, period. All they want to say is they cultivated some Black friendship, or to find out if you really do eat chitterlings, or hell, like watermelon or fried chicken, or if you can teach them how to do the bop or whatever. Just to say, "I know the Black experience". You don't know the Black experience until you live it.

This next respondent, a graduate student at a Southwestern university, gives a concrete example of the backstabbing attitudes and behaviors of Whites. It also points out the subtlety of "modern" racism. The ostensible interpretation is that the student's work was not quite up to expectations. A closer look reveals the underlying motivations for this evaluation. The student is working in the area of ethnic relations. All of a sudden, the work is inferior, not quite the quality, or not quite conforming to the "standard" of other, that is, non-ethnic, "traditional" research.

> Two faculty within my area were basically up-and-coming types who again, gave lip service to notions of equality, seemed not to really take my opinion as seriously as I thought they should have, just in terms of the research we were doing. And in fact, I received some rather negative feedback at the end of that year from those two individuals. I thought, wait a minute, I haven't heard anything like this before, nobody confronted me with anything like this my whole first year. In terms of grades, they didn't have that to complain about, in terms of my involvement in the research they didn't have that to complain about. But there was the notion that what I was doing wasn't quite good enough. It didn't conform enough to what they expected. In fact, one faculty member went so far as to suggest that I either read what he wrote or read people who he read. And this was a person who took a very narrow view of what my field ought to be about and specifically shied away from ethnic type issues. So, he was ignorant and didn't know how to deal with them. So, yea, that was a bit of a rude awakening. So, since then I've pretty much divested myself of involvement with those individuals and it's, I think that has worked for the best. Because these are people who are courteous enough but who I don't trust at a basic level, and don't really feel that comfortable dealing with.

This commentary is consistent with the general operation of a racist "standard", which views any work in the area of ethnic relations work as somehow inadequate. This student points out the shocking suddenness of the negative reviews. There was no prior indication from the "liberal" faculty members that his work was not adequate, thereby allowing him to continue with the illusion of definite progress. Then, without warning, the illusion fades and the student is stunned by the evaluations of his research. He felt betrayed and possibly even set up. On the surface, the faculty members were friendly. But, the deep layers of years of racist socialization permeated the facade. It is experiences like this that inculcate a pervading distrust of Whites among African Americans.

## Black Capitalism as Black Power

One meaning of Black Power centers on the development of African American owned and operated businesses. These businesses are primarily in the market to invest in the African American community as well as supply its wants and needs. The idea is to concentrate the enormous purchasing capacity of African Americans in their own communities. Contained in these interviews is the aspiration of many respondents to own their own businesses. They recognize the potential difficulties and have thought through strategies to overcome them.

John Sibley Butler (1991) discusses the idea of a "truncated Afro-American middleman." These African Americans come from a historical tradition that distinguishes them from the "Black bourgeoisie" of E. Franklin Frazier (1957) by their commitment to the philosophy of self-help. And, while I believe that this categorization adds an unnecessary division in an already too divided African American community, the idea is instructive. The characteristics of this concept support the idea of Black capitalism as part of the oppositional culture of African Americans. Like so many of the respondents in this study, opportunity was forged when all hope appeared gone. Butler highlights the resistance in the face of dominant oppression in the defining characteristics of this African American middleman group. This group:

> (1) adjusted to hostility by turning inward and developing economic and community institutions; (2) developed a strong tradition of family stability and excellent quality of life through housing, health care, and other means, and...
> (3) began a very strong emphasis on the importance of higher education for their offspring.

Contrary to Gordon's (1964) assessment of the Black middle class as assimilating, Butler seems to imply here that cultural values, both African and American, were transformed. This transformation created a utilitarian entrepreneurial class in response and reaction to the barriers to inclusion in the wider American society. An electronics technician living in a Western city discusses his aspirations of owning his own business. He sees this business being, firstly, the mainstay for his family and then as a positive investment for the African American community.

I would like to own my own business. That's really my main goal as far as achieving or anything like that. Like I said before, it's all back to providing for my family; that's number one in my mind. And then once I'm secure in feeling that my family's provided for, then I'd like to help other people my brothers and sisters and aunts and uncles and all down the line, and then the Black community as a whole.

An optician from a Southwestern city laments about government programs hurting the community. She stresses the importance of utilizing the resources of the African American community for the direct benefit of that community. She highlights the problem of Medicaid forcing residents out of the community to receive medical care services. This independent business owner demonstrates the need for family and community to offer support to businesses owned by African Americans in their home communities. She owed the I.R.S. ten thousand dollars and her family came up with the dollars to save the business. And, she was always encouraged by her father not to sell the business—recognizing it as a family and community asset.

The only thing that my father said to me, 'don't sell the business, you're the first Black business in the area, don't sell, you're in an excellent area.' And that just kind of swims in my head all the time to happen with me, because I wanted to sell it, it was just driving me crazy. There's nothing like the IRS telling that within thirty days you have to come up with $10,000 and you're already broke! So, fortunately my family helped me in that sense.

A highly successful business administrator speaks of becoming an entrepreneur centering on minority communities.

Ideally doing something of an entrepreneurial nature in which I might have a strong focus on the minority communities in this country. And to go back and do what I had been doing in my corporate life and what I was trained to do and what I specifically want to do and start doing that. So I just want to reestablish myself in the business community and start doing business type things and I hope to make a success of that. And not necessarily monetarily, but from a standpoint of satisfaction, knowing that you're providing a good product or a good service and that you're helping other people ideally and getting them employed and so forth.

Individual success is directly tied to community success. Most of the respondents who express the entrepreneurial spirit also insist that it is to provide for family and others in the African American community.

## Summary

The middle class African American conception of Black Power has changed since Hamilton's and Carmichael's (1964) and Hamilton's (1969) discussions of its meanings. For today's African American middle class, Black Power is advocated for the expression of African American values and ideology. Black Power can be seen in the push for Black consciousness as a means to legitimate those unique and valuable contributions to the entire American experience.

Where does the African American middle class today fall within the Black Power complex? The respondents of this sample embrace most, if not all, of the facets of Black Power. This is a sample of middle class African Americans who is strongly committed to developing aspects of Black Power dealing with Black consciousness, Black culture and heritage, Black capitalism, Black politics, and Black community control. It is further understood from these data that there is strong distrust as a result of the experiences many of these respondents have had with Whites. None of the respondents seriously suggested leaving the United States to form a new Black nation. However, the idea of separatism may be an allegorical call for autonomy. The component of violence is interesting. There seems to be an instinctive understanding and distant approval and support for instrumental violence.

There is an undertow of distrust and a fear of being "stabbed in the back" that stems from the historical treatment of African Americans as a group and also from the treatment these respondents receive as individuals from everyday racism. Black Power also manifests itself in the whole notion of Black capitalism.

This section was primarily concerned with Black consciousness, Black distrust of Whites, and Black capitalism as vehicles for the resistance to White American cultural hegemony. These three components are only the major exemplars exhibited in the present sample of respondents. And, as components of a larger dynamic, called Black Power, they represent the articulation of the continuing struggle of African Americans for liberation from oppression.

# Chapter 7
## Conclusion

This book examines the ways in which middle class African Americans experience life in contemporary American society. In depth interviews of these successful middle class respondents from all over the United States form the foundation of a reexamination of traditional paradigms of assimilation and marginality.

The data of this study suggest three immediate goals. First, an "Afrocentric sociology of race relations" is critically needed in order to understand this "minority" group. This Afrocentric perspective is based on the knowledge that the experience of African Americans is very much different from the experience of other European/White immigrants. These data demonstrate that racism and discrimination, even after the demise of legal segregation, continues to impact the lives of African Americans—even the "made-it" middle class.

Most of the respondents have faced what Philomena Essed (1990, 1991) has termed "everyday racism." The respondents give experiences of being treated poorly, not being accepted fully in the society, and being treated as second-class citizens. African Americans have made great strides toward equality; and, yet, these respondents realize their marginalized status. For example, a private practice physician cuts to the point by recognizing that class and economic levels do not guarantee inclusion for African Americans.

> I don't find it, you don't feel like you are a part of America. You always feel like you're a second-class citizen. You don't feel like you have comradeship. You're always isolated. So, from that standpoint, from a social standpoint it's hard. From an economic standpoint, it's good. In my profession, people can go to very good schools; they get a very good education. But in terms of being able to interact with society like any other person, it doesn't exist.

Similarly, a forty years old public school administrator has experienced the marginalization of second-class citizenry. She is highly educated, has her doctorate; but, she still is judged firstly by her race. She states that:

> It's difficult, even with education; you are still a second-class citizen. I have my doctorate and I have to fight to get respect everywhere. I have to demand respect. I'm constantly teaching White folk how to talk and how to act, and how to deal with me as a Black person. It is difficult.

A forty-three years old nursing supervisor whose husband is an accountant lives in an upper class, White neighborhood. Everyday racism cuts across age groups as well. She sees the isolation her twelve years old son experiences.

> Our son, within this school and environment, he feels apart, a distance, from the other children in the area. Although he socializes on an informal basis with them, in sports and that sort of thing, and in his band activities, he never actually gets invited to, say, for dinner, to go to the movies with the guys, or to do anything that may be a family kind of activity that would involve his White friends.

The experiences of these highly educated, high earning middle class African Americans demonstrate that racism is alive and well in this society. Furthermore, the racism that middle class African Americans face shapes their responses for living in this society.

The African American response to White cultural hegemony was explored. The experiences of these respondents indicate a re-fashioning of the traditional, one-way assimilation paradigm. These data indicated that American cultural patterns and values of individualism and work ethic are reconstructed into a utilitarian expression of Black Power. This expression is articulated in a unique expression of Black capitalism, Black consciousness, and an underlying distrust of Whites that is replaced by a reliance on the African American community.

The experiences of these African Americans are at once assimilated and oppositional. In the sense of assimilation, middle-class African Americans have taken on certain structural characteristics of the dominant society. But, these accommodations are adaptive survival skills. For instance, African Americans have learned the ways of White America and used this knowledge to make remarkable gains since the demise of legal segregation.

Consistent with Gordon's (1964) assessment, African Americans have acculturated to the major institutions of the dominant society. They speak "Americanized" English grammar and the outward appearance of their worship service is basically "Americanized" Christianity with the majority being members of various protestant denominations. (Lincoln and Mamiya, 1991)

However, an Afrocentric theory concerning these same experiences suggests that this stance is an adaptation to the White core cultural hegemony of American society. These middle class African Americans are adapting and changing the White culture that is forced upon them by infusing the core culture with African and African American values and principles. For example, the way that these respondents articulate the idea of Black Power demonstrates the continued value that these unique and oppositional cultural ideas and practices have in the African American community.

This research is a first attempt at allowing the voices of African Americans to speak about issues from their own experiences. These respondents tell their stories from the experiences they have lived in this society. An Afrocentric study of Black and White race relations is constructed out of these lived experiences.

Finally, over a century since Du Bois (1903) first wrote that the "problem of the dawning of the twentieth century is the problem of the color line," America still draws the distinction between races. An understanding of African

Americans from their own unique perspective is the first step in erasing the color line of oppression. Middle class African Americans feel a need for a separate perspective. They put forth a theory of experience that allows them to interpret and survive the world in which they live.

# REFERENCES

*A common destiny: Blacks and American society*, (1989). G. D. Jaynes & R. M. Williams, Jr. (Eds.). Washington, D.C.: National Academy Press.

Agresti, A. and Finlay, B. (1986). *Statistical methods for the social sciences.* (2nd ed.). San Francisco: Dellen Publishing Co.

Aptheker, H. (1943). *American negro slave revolts.* New York: Columbia University Press.

Ashmore, R. D., and Del Boca, F. K. (1981). Conceptual approaches to stereotypes and stereotyping. In D. L. Hamilton (Ed.), *Cognitive processes in stereotyping and intergroup behavior,* (pp. 1-35). Hillsdale, NJ: Lawrence Erlbaum Associates.

Babbie, E. (1983). *The Practice of social research.* (3rd ed.). Belmont, CA: Wadsworth Publishing Co.

Baker, H. A. (1992). *Workings of the spirit: The poetics of Afro-American women's writing.* Chicago: University of Chicago Press.

Bastide, R. (1971). *African civilisations in the new world.* New York: Harper & Row.

Bellah, R. N., Madsen, R., Sullivan, W. M., Swidler, A., and Tipton, S. M. (1985). *Habits of the heart: Individualism and commitment in American life.* New York: Harper & Row.

Benjamin, L. (1991). *The Black elite: Facing the color line in the twilight of the twentieth century.* Chicago: Nelson-Hall, Inc.

Bennett, L., Jr. (1961). *Before the Mayflower: A history of the Negro in America 1619-1964.* Baltimore: Penguin Books.

Berger, P. L., and Luckmann, T. (1977). *The social construction of reality: A treatise in the sociology of knowledge.* New York: Anchor Books.

Blauner, R. (1972). *Racial oppression in America.* New York: Harper & Row.

Bonacich, E. (1976). Advanced capitalism and Black/White race relations in the United States: A split labor market interpretation. *American Sociological Review, 41,* (February), pp. 34-51.

Burawoy, M. (1991). *Ethnography unbound: Power and resistance in the modern metropolis.* Berkeley: University of California Press.

Butler, J. S. (1992). *Entrepreneurship and self-help among Black Americans: A reconstruction of race and economics.* Albany, NY: State University of New York Press.

Carmichael, S., and Hamilton, C. V. (1967). *Black power: The politics of liberation in America.* New York: Random House.

Cox, O. C. (1948). *Caste, class and race: A study in social dynamics.* New York: Monthly Review Press.

Du Bois, W. E. B. (1903). The souls of Black folk. In *Three Negro Classics.* New York: Avon Books.

——— (1935). *Black reconstruction.* New York: Harcourt, Brace & Co.

——— (1973). *The education of Black people: Ten critiques, 1906-1960.* Herbert Aptheker (Ed.). New York: Monthly Review Press.

Early, Kevin (1992). *Religion and Suicide in the African-American Community.* West Port, CT: Greenwood Press.

Essed, P. (1990). *Everyday racism: Reports from women of two cultures.* Claremont, CA: Hunter House, Inc.

——— (1991). *Understanding everyday racism: An interdisciplinary theory.* London: Sage Publications.

Feagin, J. R., and Feagin, C. B. (1978). *Discrimination American style: Institutional racism and sexism*, (2nd ed.). Malabar, FL: Robert E. Krieger Publishing Co.

——— (1990). *Social problems: A critical power-conflict perspective*, (3rd ed.). Englewood Cliffs, NJ: Prentice-Hall.

Feagin, J. R. (1989). *Racial and ethnic relations*, (3rd ed.). Englewood Cliffs, NJ: Prentice Hall.

——— (1991). The continuing significance of race: Anti-Black discrimination in public places.*American Sociological Review, 56*(February), pp. 101-116.

Fine, G. A. (1990). Symbolic interactionism in the post-Blumerian age. In G. Ritzer (ed.), *Frontiers in social theory.* New York: Columbia University Press.

Franklin, J. H., and Moss, A. A., Jr. (1989). *From slavery to freedom: A history of Negro Americans.* 6th ed. New York: McGraw-Hill.

Frazier, E. F. (1957). *Black bourgeoisie.* New York: Free Press.

Galtung, J. (1967). *Theory and methods of social research.* New York: Columbia University Press.

Gans, H. J. (1988). *Middle American individualism: The future of liberal democracy.* New York: Free Press.

Glaser, B. G. and Strauss, A. L. (1967). *The discovery of grounded theory: Strategies for qualitative research.* New York: Aldine De Gruyter.

Glazer, N., and Moynihan, D. P. (1963). *Beyond the melting pot: The Negroes, Puerto Ricans, Jews, Italians, and Irish of New York city.* Cambridge, MA: The M.I.T. Press.

Gleason, P. (1980). American identity and Americanization. In *Harvard encyclopedia of American ethnic groups,* Thernstrom, S., Orlov, A., and Handlin, O. (Eds.), pp. 31-58. Cambridge, MA: Harvard University Press.

Gordon, M. M. (1964). *Assimilation in American life: The role of race, religion, and national origin.* New York: Oxford University Press.

Gramsci, A. (1971). *Selections from the prison notebooks.* New York: International Publishers.

Greeley, A. M. (1974). *Ethnicity in the United States: A preliminary reconnaissance.* New York: John Wiley & Sons.

Hamilton, C. V. (1969). *Urban violence.* Chicago: University of Chicago Press.

# References

Hechter, M. (1975). *Internal colonialism.* Berkeley: University of California Press.
Herskovits, M. J. (1941/1958). *The myth of the Negro past.* Boston, MA: Beacon Press.
Holloway, J. E. (Ed.), (1990). *Africanisms in American culture.* Bloomington, IN: Indiana University Press.
Kitano, H. H. L. (1991). *Race relations.* 4th ed. Englewood Cliffs, NJ: Prentice Hall.
Landry, B. (1987). *The new Black middle class.* Berkeley, CA: University of California Press.
Levine, L. W. (1977). *Black culture and Black consciousness: Afro-American thought from slavery to freedom.* New York: Oxford University Press.
Lincoln, C. E., and Mamiya, L. H. (1990). *The Black church in the African American experience.* Durham, NC: Duke University Press.
Lippmann, W. (1922). *Public opinion.* New York: Harcourt, Brace and Co.
Lurie, N. O. (1982). The American Indian: Historical background. In Yetman, N. R. and Steele, C. H. (Eds.), *Majority and Minority,* (3rd. ed.). (pp. 131-144). New York: Allyn and Bacon.
Marable, M. (1984). *Race, reform and rebellion: The second reconstruction in Black America, 1945-1982.* Jackson, MS: University Press of Mississippi.
McAdoo, H. (1981). *Black families.* Beverly Hills, CA: Sage Publications.
McLemore, S. D. (1991). *Racial and ethnic relations in America,* (3rd ed.). Boston, MA: Allyn and Bacon.
Myrdal, G. (1944). *An American dilemma.* New York: Harper and Brothers.
Park, R. E. and Burgess, E. W. (1921). *Introduction to the science of sociology.* Chicago: University of Chicago Press.
Pinkney, A. (1984). *The myth of Black progress.* New York: Cambridge University Press.
Schermerhorn, R. A. (1970). *Comparative ethnic relations.* New York: Random House.
Scott, J. (1990). *Domination and the arts of resistance: Hidden transcripts.* New Haven, CT: Yale University Press.
Sowell, T. (1975). *Affirmative action reconsidered: Was it necessary in academia?* Washington, DC: American Enterprise Institute for Public Policy Research.
——— (1987). *A conflict of visions: Ideological origins of political struggles.* New York: Quill, William Morrow.
Staples, R. (1976). *Introduction to Black sociology.* New York: McGraw-Hill Book Company.
Steele, S. (1990). *The content of our character: A new vision of race in America.* New York: St. Martin's Press.
Stonequist, E. (1937). *The marginal man: A study in personality and culture conflict.* New York: C. Scribner's Sons.

Tajfel, H. (1969). Cognitive aspects of prejudice. *Journal of Social Issues, 25*, 79-97.

Wallerstein, I. (1983). *Historical capitalism*. London: Verso.

Weber, M. (1958). *The protestant ethic and the spirit of capitalism: The relationships between religion and the economic and social life in modern culture*. New York: Charles Scribner's Sons.

Yetman, N. R. (1985). *Majority and minority: The dynamics of race and ethnicity in American life*. Boston, MA: Allyn and Bacon.

Yette, S. F. (1971). *The choice: The issue of Black survival in America*. Silver Spring, MD: Cottage Books.

# Index

## A

African American cultural opposition, ix
Afrocentric, viii, ix, 1, 3, 4, 7, 9, 10, 17, 20, 25, 28, 31, 55, 70, 79, 80
American core culture, viii, 2, 9, 11, 17, 33, 40, 51, 59, 60, 65, 70
anglicizing, 2
Anglicizing
see assimilation, 42
Anglo conformity, viii, 2, 7, 9, 25, 30, 32, 33, 34, 55, 60, 70, 71
assimilation, vii, viii, 2, 3, 4, 7, 8, 9, 11, 12, 16, 17, 24, 25, 26, 27, 28, 30, 31, 32, 33, 34, 35, 36, 37, 40, 45, 47, 48, 49, 60, 67, 70, 72, 79, 80
assimilation paradigm. *See* assimilation process
assimilation process, vii, viii, 2, 7, 9, 16, 25, 26, 31, 33, 35, 36, 37, 47, 49, 72
Assimiliation, 7, 9, 10, 25, 26, 32, 33, 34, 35, 84
attribution processes, 5
misattribution, 5

## B

Black power, 68, 83
Black Power, ix, 68, 69, 71, 72, 75, 76, 77, 80

## C

core American culture, vii, 2
core American values, ix
cultural hegemony, ix, 68, 77, 80
cultural pluralism, viii, 2, 7, 9, 25, 32
Cultural pluralism, 32
cultural resistance, ix, 71

## D

discrimination, vii, viii, 2, 11, 12, 13, 16, 18, 19, 20, 21, 22, 23, 24, 28, 33, 35, 38, 39, 42, 43, 48, 55, 67, 72, 79, 84
Discrimination, 47, 84
dominant culture, vii, 1, 10, 11, 39, 40, 45, 61, 70, 71, 74

## E

Eurocentric, vii, 3

## I

individualism
American Core Culture, ix, 25, 39, 51, 52, 53, 54, 55, 59, 62, 65, 80, 84

## J

Jim-Crow. *See* segregation

## M

marginal, vii, viii, 2, 8, 36, 38, 39, 40, 45, 49, 85

marginal personality hypothesis, vii, 2
marginality, viii, ix, 2, 3, 4, 7, 8, 10, 38, 39, 42, 43, 45, 46, 47, 48, 49, 65, 79
melting pot ideal, 2, 10
melting pot ideology, viii, 30

## N

neo-conservative, viii, 1, 16, 20

## O

oppositional culture, viii, 4, 67, 75
organic intellectuals, 9, 28

## P

peripheral, vii, 2, 42

## R

race relations cycle, vii, 3, 9
  accommodation, 3
  competition, 3, 53
  contacts, 3
racialized, 11, 18, 53, 57
racism, vii, ix, 1, 2, 9, 10, 11, 12, 14, 15, 18, 19, 20, 21, 22, 24, 28, 29, 32, 38, 39, 42, 43, 44, 46, 55, 67, 72, 74, 77, 79, 80, 84
rationality
  American Core Culture, ix, 25, 39, 45

## S

segregation
  de jure, 1, 2, 12, 13, 28, 33, 37, 42, 47, 55, 79, 80
stereotyping, vii, 39, 40, 71, 83
strong work ethic, ix, 51, 53, 55, 59, 65
subordinate group, vii, 1

## W

White cultural hegemony, ix, 46, 69, 80

# Biography

Michael E. Hodge received his M.S. in psychology and his Ph.D. in sociology from the University of Florida. He has taught at the University of Georgia, University of Tennessee, and Georgia State University. He is currently an associate professor at Morehouse College and a research associate with the Research Center on Health Disparities. His areas of interest focus on racial and ethnic inequality, including health disparities as well as socioeconomic inequity. He is currently analyzing data collected from in-depth interviews of college age African Americans concerning risky sexual activity in an age of HIV/AIDS. He served as president of the Georgia Sociological Association 2008-09). He is a Life-Time Member of the Association of Black Sociologists and has served on several committees within the organization.

Hodge is married with two children and resides in a southern suburb of Atlanta.